Alchemy for t

Praise for *Alchemy for the Mind: Create Your Confident Core*

I loved this book — it's right up my street. It's inspiring, informative and easy to read. A concise, detailed and easy to absorb explanation of the mind–body loop and the inescapable impact that it has on our efficiency as human beings — both negative and positive. There's enough science in Alchemy For The Mind to teach and inform yet not so much as to overwhelm. If developing a confident core is high on your agenda, then this book will help to get you there.

Wilma Allan, The Money Midwife

Confidence is such a complex issue and Rhian has done a fantastic job of bringing together all the key points in an accessible and engaging format. The book clearly shows you why confidence is a big issue and how it affects our lives. I love the way she has written it, with lots of interesting facts, reinforced through the inclusion of stories about her own experiences and those of her clients. It's a fascinating subject, well presented, which kept me turning the pages. I love Part III for the numerous strategies included, which I will try. For me, awareness is one the biggest things I teach my own clients and this book does just that. A great read if you are suffering from a lack of confidence or even if you want to become more aware for others. The book flowed seamlessly which made it not only interesting but enjoyable. A great read.

Ann Dobbs, Freedom to Fly

I was interested in this book since I wanted to address my lack of confidence in dealing with conflict and challenging situations. Following the strategies has made it clear that for me, confidence really means being myself. This has been so helpful in changing how I feel. The descriptions of the brain and how we can relearn how to respond have inspired me to make real changes and I am enjoying the confidence this is bringing me.

Samantha, a client

Alchemy for the Mind

Create Your Confident Core

by Rhian Sherrington

Practical Inspiration Publishing
2014

First published in Great Britain 2014 by Practical Inspiration Publishing

© Rhian Sherrington 2014

The moral rights of the author have been asserted.

ISBN (print): 978-1-910056-06-6
ISBN (ebook): 978-1-910056-07-3

Table of Contents

Part 3: Strategies

About the Author

Rhian Sherrington is a Personal Performance Coach based in Bristol, UK. Her passion is enabling professional women to enhance their lives through overcoming procrastination, fear and frustration. Using her perceptive and intuitive approach, clients are able to enjoy newly found beliefs and behaviours that allow them to flourish.

The information and strategies contained in this book bring together Rhian's expertise in behaviour change, people management and coaching. She also draws upon her personal journey and the tools she has used to develop her own confident core. Before establishing Choose2Flourish, her coaching and training business, Rhian was a successful senior manager for an environmental charity and has worked as an adviser for the UK Government. Earlier in her career she ran her own expeditions company and taught geography and environmental studies.

Always the avid learner, Rhian holds a degree from Oxford University, a Masters in Environmental Management and further Diplomas in Personal Performance Coaching, Corporate & Executive Coaching and Training & Development. She enjoys keeping up to date with neuroscience and positive psychology to inform and support her coaching practice. She loves Qi Gong, surfing, and family cycling and walking adventures, especially when they involve picnics in wild and beautiful places.

Rhian Sherrington

Choose2Flourish Ltd
22 West Mall
Clifton
Bristol
BS8 4BQ

Dedication

This book is dedicated to everyone out there who suffers from low confidence. Trust that you can build a confident core that will always be there for you, allowing you to flourish, at work, at home, in life.

It is also dedicated to my children, Murray and Megan. May you always know and believe in yourselves.

Acknowledgments

It takes courage to admit to yourself that you want to change your life and improve aspects of yourself. I've been lucky enough to work with some amazing clients who wanted to, and have achieved just that. Their stories included here provide a wonderful testament to what can happen when you choose to change what you believe about yourself.

This book would have remained on my 'someday' list if it hadn't have been for the support and encouragement of my husband Chris. His diligent proofreading improved the flow of my writing and for all those late nights when he was faced with yet more chapters to read instead of heading off to bed, I can't thank him enough.

My gratitude also goes to Sam Neffendorf, Laura Doulton and Nicky Marshall for their enthusiasm for, and fantastic contributions to, this book.

Finally, my eternal thanks to Alison Jones, of Practical Inspiration Publishing, for all her coaching and support in transforming my embryonic idea to a fully-fledged publication. I couldn't have done it without her.

Client Confidentiality
All clients mentioned in this book have had their names changed in order to protect coach–client confidentiality.

Contributors

Confidence and Emotional Freedom Technique

Sam Neffendorf loves to empower people to overcome the limiting emotional states and self-belief issues that stand in the way of them achieving true freedom and happiness in their life. He is an advanced practitioner of EFT, Matrix Re-imprinting and Birth Re-imprinting and, as a skilled and intuitive listener, is very gently able to support his clients to uncover and move through the blocks that are causing them to feel trapped, victimised or display other recurring limiting patterns. For more information, visit his website: www.freedomhereandnow.com.

Confidence and Personal Image

Laura Doulton is passionate about working with women to help them look and feel fabulous, to enable them to reach their full potential and flourish in every sense. She runs an image consultancy based in Bristol offering the following services:

- Colour analysis
- Personal styling
- Wardrobe organisation
- Personal shopping

She also gives talks for both professional and social women's networking groups, and runs group workshops.

Laura Doulton Image Consultancy
22 West Mall,
Clifton,
Bristol,
BS8 4BQ
E: laura@lauradoulton.com
www.lauradoulton.com

Confidence and State Management
Nicky Marshall is an author, speaker
and mentor. Nicky has combined her fi-
nance and accounting background with
her training in the wellbeing and stress
management industry to create her Discover Your Bounce® programmes.

Designed to eliminate stress, create wellbeing and encourage a positive
attitude in business and life, Discover
Your Bounce is available in a variety
of formats including Discover Your
Bounce in the Workplace for compa-
nies. Nicky's programmes and workshops are informative, inspiring and
fun!

Nicky is passionate about well-being and loves to encourage her at-
tendees to change their lives for the better. For more information and to
download her free eBook visit: discoveryourbounce.com.

Part 1

Overview

Optimism is the faith that leads to achievement. Nothing can be done without hope and confidence.

Helen Keller

1

What is the Confident Core?

Research indicates that lack of confidence is *the* biggest factor holding back women in their careers. Why this should be the case is not completely understood, although the influences of social and cultural norms in childhood are likely be contributing factors. How we educate children, the delicate process of building self-efficacy beliefs (e.g. 'I can do it!'), the impact of personal situations and motivation, all form part of the mix. Whatever the causes, if you feel you lack confidence, you are in very good company. There are a lot of women (and some men) out there who feel the same and this is damaging their careers, as well as affecting the quality of their relationships and other aspects of their lives.

Do You Lack Confidence?

Do you ever find yourself wondering why you can feel the most confident woman in the world when speaking with your close friends but when it comes to complaining about something or standing up for yourself in public, you stay quiet and then fume about it for hours afterwards? Maybe the confident you is there in business, at work, but evaporates when you're out socially or when you find yourself in uncharted territory such as being with new people or in a stressful situation.

Perhaps you can readily present your arguments to your team or close peers but when it comes to speaking up with senior colleagues or an individual you find challenging, your pulse races, you can't find the right words and you miss the opportunity to get your voice heard.

Maybe you believe you can never really show your true self — that the person you are is not someone who is confident, who can ever be confident? As a result you've stayed quiet, played small and suffered through many situations where you would have liked to have done something, or said something, but never did.

Perhaps you *had* confidence and then someone, or something, robbed you of it. You had a knock, a setback, in a relationship, at work, in your studies. Things happen that upend us, such as the death of someone close to us or a humiliating experience. Loss of face, loss of financial security, divorce, creeping debt, not being to get a job or being made redundant — all of these things can make us question our abilities and lose faith in ourselves.

You may of course be at the other end of the spectrum. Perhaps outwardly you appear very confident, always ready to express your opinion. Inwardly, however, you're very unsure, using bravado and humour to avoid having to expose a rather more vulnerable, less confident you.

Whether you experience what I call *'fluctuating confidence'* or a belief that you never have confidence, *Alchemy for the Mind: Create Your Confident Core* has been written especially for you. Don't suffer this limiting influence in your life any more. It is your birth right to feel that sense of freedom and joy that comes from truly being you. You don't have to suffer the constriction of life experience nor the crippling sense of regret and other negative emotions that rise from not feeling confident enough to be yourself.

This book has been written for everyone who thinks they don't have the confidence to achieve what their heart desires. My aim is to show you how we can be the creators of our own minds and bring about the alchemy, the inner transformation, to build a confident core.

Sometimes we can confuse a lack of confidence with low self-esteem. There is an important distinction though between the two. Self-esteem is an emotional sense of self-worth. If you lack self-esteem, your introspection is negative, you don't believe you are capable of much and you see yourself as inadequate, unworthy, unlovable. This negativity permeates every thought, resulting in faulty assumptions and self-sabotaging behaviours. If self-esteem is what you really need to explore, this book and the strategies described in Part III are still for you, but I would invite you to consider what personal, bespoke support you might benefit from as well.

In *Alchemy for the Mind: Create Your Confident Core* we're going to explore various ways of considering how you can build a confident core by re-programming your mind and consciously choosing to believe there is a different you waiting to appear. I'm very grateful for, and delighted to be able to include, contributions from three experts, Sam Neffendorf, Nicky Marshall and Laura Dolton, each of whom has some excellent and amazing perspectives, tools and tips to share with you in order to help you create the inner transformation that you are seeking. I'm also going to share with you ten strategies for re-programming your mind to truly become the confident, beautiful human being that is waiting to emerge. Changing how confident you feel won't happen overnight, but change it you can — the brain science and holistic mind-body understanding is out there to prove it!

A Confident Core: Why does it matter?

In a survey of 3,000 managers in 2011, the Institute of Leadership and Management (ILM) found there was significant difference in career confidence between men and women (2011). Female managers showed lower levels of personal confidence and higher levels of self-doubt compared to their male counterparts, which combined to create significant barriers to career progression. Across the age groups, 70% of male managers had high or quite high levels of confidence, compared to 50% of women. Half of all women managers surveyed also reported feelings of self-doubt, compared to only 30% of men. Furthermore the research found there was a strong link between confidence levels and ambition. Higher levels of confidence coupled with a very clear idea of career path led to higher expectations of advancement. Women with low confidence were the least likely to achieve their career ambitions.

Your competence, especially your perceived competence, is closely connected to your level of confidence. The two are linked together in a self-feeding loop, which can flow in both a negative and positive way. If you have self-confidence, you're more likely to have a positive belief in, and judgement of, your abilities. Your 'perceived competence', that is your self-assessment of your ability in performing a specific activity or job properly, is likely to be high. This has real bearing on how women (and men) can get on in the world as we all pick up on 'projected confidence'. This is the ability to instil confidence of your competence in others. It is natural for people to interpret a confident manner as evidence of being good at something. That may not be correct or fair, but if you believe you are competent and are able to project confidence, you are more likely to be perceived as capable and to be trusted by others. Having a confident core therefore, simply helps you to get on in life!

You may like to note at this point a curious effect that social psychologists Dunning and Kruger (1999) identified in their research. They discovered an inverse correlation between confidence and competence, sometimes referred to as the 'Paradox of Confidence' or the 'Dunning-Kruger Effect'. This is the opposite of what most of us might assume given our natural tendency to ascribe competence to confident people. Put more bluntly, the unintelligent get confident while the intelligent get doubtful, or in the words of Bertrand Russell:

> *One of the painful things about our time is that that those who feel certainty are stupid and those with any imagination and understanding are filled with doubt and indecision.*

Putting this together with the research undertaken by the ILM, it may be tempting to suggest that if you are a highly competent, intelligent woman, then you are more likely to feel less confident and therefore less likely to inspire others to believe in you and consequently less likely to succeed. While this conclusion might be too strongly worded the research does suggest that there are real barriers facing those who are and are perceived to be, lacking in confidence.

Low confidence can be severely crippling, holding you back from the success, recognition and fulfilment you deserve. In the most recent survey of life satisfaction across EU countries, people in the UK rated their competence very low, which had a negative effect on their overall levels of satisfaction in life. Believing yourself to be less competent than you are therefore has a wider impact than whether you advance in your career. It can actually affect the extent to which you are able to thrive and flourish in your life.

Having confidence gives you freedom of choice and action. If you believe yourself to be capable of new and amazing things, you are able to keep building a sense of accomplishment and satisfaction in your life. In Martin Seligman's illuminating book, *Flourish* (2011), he highlighted the importance of accomplishment to our long-term health and well-being. Seligman sees the ability to keep learning and pushing ourselves forward, overcoming what was once challenging and developing new skills, as vital, one of his five 'pillars' to a flourishing life. In doing so, we feel more positive, which in turn, as I explain later, helps open up our cognitive abilities even further, expanding the likelihood for even more accomplishment and satisfaction. Conquering what was once hard builds confidence. Just think back for a moment to that last thing you accomplished, perhaps something you once found daunting but you went ahead and achieved it anyway. How does that feel inside?

When I first started my coaching business, I felt terribly exposed. I had been used to standing up and representing the organisation I was working for confidently and competently, at international conferences, on the radio (including an interview on Jeremy Vine's lunchtime show on Radio 2), and on TV. Expressing myself was far from a problem — I enjoyed it and thrived on it. Changing to a situation where I was now talking about and promoting my business and therefore myself was completely different. Standing up in front of networking groups, I was totally taken over by 'amygdala hijack'. This is when part of the brain, the amygdala, senses a potential threat and switches on the fear response. Amongst other things, this releases cortisol into the bloodstream, raises the pulse and switches blood flow away from the brain towards the extremities (to get ready to run), which reduces cognitive abilities and generally makes you feel dreadful.

At the heart of the difference between the 'employed' and 'self-employed' me was that I perceived myself to be 'on my own' in a new role that I just didn't feel confident about. This was generating feelings of anxiety, and if I examine that a little more deeply, I can sense added layers of frustration (with myself for not being more confident) and a fear of being negatively judged. All of these are stressors, triggering the negative emotions that trip the mind-body into the 'amygdala hijack' described above. My confident core had not survived the transition from employee to self-employed and I knew I urgently needed to invest in myself again to rebuild what I had come to know, and rely on, in myself.

Not feeling confident creates stress — a mental and bodily tension. In the short term, lacking confidence, succumbing to amygdala hijack or enduring an emotional landscape based around anxiety is going to limit your personal effectiveness and prevent you from fully expressing yourself in a way that brings satisfaction, meaning and a sense of accomplishment. Some level of stress in our lives is helpful, essential even. This 'eustress' is a positive stress and is what drives us to meet our deadlines and goals. Without it, we might never find the motivation, energy and drive to fulfil our potential. However, in the long term, experiencing negative stress, 'distress', can be highly damaging to our health and well-being. For example, excessive exposure to cortisol (the chemical released when the 'fight/ flight' response has been stimulated) has been linked to life-limiting conditions such as cardiovascular disease, cancer, diabetes, peptic ulcers and mental illness, such as depression.

By working through the strategies outlined in Part III of this book, I have successfully re-built my inner confident core since those first scary months of 'flying solo'. My clients have also re-discovered, or created anew, a solid core of confidence which has been instrumental in allowing them to dream big again, find their voice, achieve their goals and flourish in their lives.

Having confidence empowers us to choose nourishing relationships, with ourselves and with others. It enables us to speak our truth, to stand up for what we believe in. We are able to follow our hearts, to take responsibility for ourselves and ensure there is a match between our values and what we think, what we say and what we do. Creating a confident core inside means always being able to trust yourself, your decisions and intuition. You can say no and mean it, without any guilt. It helps you prioritise and stop procrastinating.

So, make a stand for yourself. Draw that line in the sand knowing that you have the power within you to change your story, to create that solid core of confidence that will then empower you to create a beautiful, meaningful and flourishing life. I invite you to open your hearts, and your minds, and read on.

A Small Health Warning and a Disclaimer

It's important that you're aware of what beliefs you are holding about yourself before we move any further. **Do you believe you can change how you currently are?** If you really don't, then this book is not going to help you very much. I do hope though, that by buying this book, you have a sense that you *can* help yourself to change — because, I, along with many, many others, believe, and know, that you can.

You should also be aware that a severe lack of confidence in social situations, a fear of negative appraisal, along with severe physical symptoms that lead to avoidance of social situations, is social phobia or social anxiety. This can be addressed through a diagnosable type of treatment, such as cognitive behaviour therapy. If you find your symptoms are severe, a trip to the GP in the first instance is a priority.

2

My Story

I'm Rhian Sherrington, Personal Performance and Corporate Coach, facilitator, mother, life traveller and change maker. I use my insights and understanding to enable others to find the courage and confidence to make the changes needed to flourish at work, at home, in life. I'm particularly passionate about working with experienced women professionals to re-programme thoughts, beliefs and behaviours that no longer serve them. Fundamental to stepping up into their authentic self, and truly flourishing, is the ability to find their voice, claim their confidence and use their courage. I've been called a 'Life Alchemist', as not only have I changed my own life, I've helped many others find their own way forward to positively transform their lives for the better.

It has taken me many years to fully own, and use, my strengths, and to find the voice inside me that has always wanted to emerge. My block? A lack of confidence and self-belief that wouldn't permit me to speak my truth and be truly me. Even with the benefit of a great education, with a first degree from Oxford University followed by a Master's degree, and even though I've led and participated in expeditions to North

East Greenland, Northern Pakistan and Ecuador, I always felt very unsure about myself. During my twenties, I lost myself in unhelpful, toxic romantic relationships that had a very damaging impact on how I saw myself and what I believed about myself. Things improved markedly as I approached thirty, arising from the time and support I had invested to re-programme unhelpful thoughts and beliefs that were holding me back. My life improved considerably and from the outside at least, you would have thought I had got it all worked out at long last.

Jump forward a decade to three years ago when I was turning 40 and working as a behaviour change specialist in the environmental sector. Having worked my way up, I was feeling proud of having finally reached a place where I could make a real contribution and work part time, having a son who was just into school and a two-year-old daughter. That inner work I'd done over the years had certainly helped to overcome my default setting of uncertainty about the world and my abilities, but I still suffered from fluctuating confidence that would sabotage me at times.

Despite the good salary and a certain sense of accomplishment, a feeling of rising disquiet, that things weren't quite right, bubbled away, half noticed, inside. When on maternity leave with my daughter I had declared to my mother-in-law that within a year I would be doing something very different in the way of work. But there I was, getting more entrenched within a career that whilst meaningful, was very stressful. I didn't feel able to be myself, in fact I wasn't really tuned in to who that was. Outside of work, however, my life was very rewarding. I was, and remain, very happily married and our family was settling in well into our very own self-built eco-home. Exploring a change of career direction, however, seemed financially impossible, let alone the self-belief, time and energy I knew it would require.

That was until the unthinkable happened. My wonderful brother-in-law, Tom, my husband's brother, took his own life. Out of the shock and heartbreak came the deep realisation that I was actually deeply unhappy in work and more than just stagnating, I was being suffocated. My values were no longer being met and I was struggling to get my real voice heard. Suddenly I could no longer tolerate it and wanted the freedom to focus on what I knew I was good at — listening to people, helping them work their way through problems, inspiring and motivating them to make changes, guiding them to learn. I had intuitively felt Tom's confusion and had tried to help him, as had many of his family and friends, but there was no way we could have foreseen his desperate, dark thoughts as he never shared them. Working through my own sense of guilt and grief, I've had to use all my courage to carefully cultivate a far stronger core of confidence. Knowing I needed to step away from my old career,

I've embraced the new, fuller, more authentic me that was ready now to emerge.

It's been a fascinating journey so far, re-training as a professional coach and combining all my knowledge and expertise around how we can change our behaviour and build resilience in ourselves, drawing together my interests in neuroscience, mind–body connections and positive transition. As a Life Alchemist, I now combine what we know about how the brain works with the mystery and joy of inner transformation to enable others to truly flourish. I whole-heartedly believe that life is too short to sit in the wings. Take a deep breath and step out onto your stage.

I do hope you enjoy this book and find it useful in your life journey. If you take just one thing away from reading it, remember this:

I believe that only those who claim their confidence can truly flourish in life. Make that you.

3

Defining Alchemy for the Mind

How do you view your mind?

Is it something that you believe you have very little influence over, or do you recognise the gap that exists between a stimulus and your response that allows you to choose how you react to any particular thought or circumstance? Do you see your life as something you can fully create by influencing what you think and believe, or do you see everything as being outside of your control? I ask these questions because how you answer is fundamental to how you're going to respond to thinking about 'Alchemy for the Mind'.

Your brain is made up of around 100 billion nerve cells (called neurons) forming over a trillion connections (or synapses) that are in a constant dynamic state, understanding and interpreting the world around you. Everything you see, hear, feel, everything you experience, has been created by your brain especially for you. This leads to an interesting question of whether you see yourself as your brain's creator, leader and teacher or if you regard your brain as being in charge. In *Super Brain: Unleash the explosive power of your mind*, Deepak Chopra and Rudolph

E Tanzi (2013) put forward a powerful argument that when you step up and acknowledge that it isn't your genes that control how your brain works, but you, you can use that awareness to create a 'super brain' that will become your gateway to a future that maximises health, happiness and spiritual well-being.

In my own life and when working with my clients as a professional coach, I've witnessed first-hand the power of transforming what we think, believe and subsequently do. I would never have led my own expedition to Ecuador or rebuilt my life after a failed relationship, if I hadn't accepted that I had a choice as to how I viewed my future. That choice involved learning to develop a state of mind that built my confidence.

I remember one client, Alice, whom I met early on in my coaching days. She was really struggling to see herself as someone who could, for example, go to a dance class on her own or go running on her own. Her confidence was very, very low. In bite-sized steps, she learnt to re-programme those limiting beliefs about herself in such a way that she was able not only to go running but to start to feel confident about herself in other situations, such as getting a job she really wanted but which she lacked the confidence to go for. By the time we finished working together, Alice was successfully ensconced in a new fulfilling role and was able to seek out new opportunities to build her social circle and was running regularly, on her own. In so doing, Alice reclaimed the creator, teacher and leadership role over her own mind, becoming her own 'alchemist' to change her thoughts, beliefs and behaviour.

So to start, let's get clear on what 'alchemy' is so you can see how applying an 'Alchemy for the Mind' approach is going to help you build that confident core.

What is Alchemy?

Alchemy has a long tradition, going way back to the Ancient Greeks. The word itself is late Middle English, via Old French and Medieval Latin, which itself comes from the Arabic — al-kīmyā, the 'al' meaning 'the' and kīmyā coming from the Greek — khēmia — the art of transmuting metals. As a Medieval forerunner of chemistry, alchemy was concerned with attempting to convert base metals into gold (or silver) and finding a universal elixir that would confer youth and longevity. Alchemy is recognised as a 'protoscience' that contributed to the development of modern chemistry and medicine, through its development of a structure of basic laboratory techniques, theories, terminology and experimental method.

Alongside this physical, tangible aspect of the Alchemist's work was also a more esoteric thread. This thread was a seemingly magical process of transformation, of creation or combination. Alchemy differs from modern science in that included within its approach were practices taken from religion, magic and mythology. There is an essential, internal aspect to alchemy — that of an inner transformation that occurs through a guided, but somewhat magical process. The key point to remember here is that alchemy is a process that creates a transformation into something more beautiful, purer and somehow more evolved than was there before. Whilst the alchemy of old has been long superseded by science and medicine as they developed into their modern forms, the core idea of inner transformation, of following a process for inner, empowering change has been retained and refined in the holistic 'mind–body' disciplines.

What I put forward here in *Alchemy for the Mind* is that this is something you can learn; there are processes you can follow through which you can enjoy an empowering inner transformation that creates a fuller, more authentic you. *Alchemy for the Mind* also includes a call for openness, to trying on something new: experiment a little and see how by choosing to change the way you see things, you can access far more wisdom and meaning than ever before. Like the Alchemists of old, having a little faith that something bigger than you is out there, helping you on your journey, goes a long way to supporting you as you embark on your internal transformation.

What is 'The Mind'?

The relationship between our brain and our mind, and specifically the question of how separate or unified these two entities are, has been debated since the time of the early Egyptians. In the 'mind versus brain' discussion, the question of whether the mind is completely 'created' by the brain is something that has still not been resolved. The spiritual dimension, that there is something greater than the individual mind, perhaps a shared consciousness, of which we are all part, is an important aspect of that debate. Whilst many experts explain consciousness solely as a consequence of the complex electrical, chemical and physical feedback loops between the brain and body, numerous eminent physicists, neuroscientists and brain surgeons in an expanding field of research argue, along with intuitive and spiritual leaders, that we are indeed all part of the same universal consciousness. Of course what each of us decides to believe is a matter of personal choice. I simply invite you to keep an open mind and register what resonates with you as you read further.

Neuroplasticity

For more than 400 years the brain was considered by medical science to be something of a machine, with different parts doing specific jobs, which deteriorated over time until all its functions eventually stop working. This has now been shown not to be the case. Whilst dead cells can't be repaired, the brain can grow new cells and continue to grow — 'use it or lose it' being a common and somewhat appropriate refrain. Developments in scanning technology, such as MRI and fMRI scans that allow us to see brain structure and activity respectively, have enabled us to understand like never before what is going on inside the living brain.

The brain is comprised of between 90 and 100 billion neurons, the 'working cells' of the brain. These information-processing cells are made up of a core nucleus, a long slender fibre, called the axon and short extensions called dendrites. Neurons are physically separate from each other and communication occurs via 'synapses', the junction between the axon of one neuron and the dendrite of another. This communication can happen either chemically via neurotransmitters or electrically. This mix of electrical and chemical activity results in a connection being made between neurons. Repeated transmission or connection between neurons causes them to 'fire off' together so that over repeated firing they 'wire together'. This is how neural pathways are formed in the brain.

Neuroplasticity means the development of pathways in the brain. Traditionally, the early years of life and puberty, leading into the early 20s, were seen as key years of brain growth and development. After that, it was commonly believed that we all endure a slow but relentless process of gentle deterioration. The unexpected recovery of function in stroke and brain injury patients however, has led to a re-appraisal of this belief. In this emerging science, we now know that the brain is able to develop new pathways throughout life. So whilst damaged or dead brain cells can't be brought back to life, new brain cells can be developed through neurogenesis. The brain can therefore develop new ways of thinking and behaving, meaning that we can change our neural pathways and learn different behaviours, different habits. We now know that an adult brain is capable of changing as a result of experience. As the effects of psychotherapy demonstrate, revisiting emotionally charged experiences through reframing, and reappraisal, can create a different, more positive state of mind. The influence of mindfulness practices on the brain has also shown positive changes to brain function and structure, not to mention the effects on mental well-being and social life.

The important thing to note is this: by bringing awareness to how you feel and how you think, you are taking the first step towards being the alchemist for your mind. If you believe you are the creator of your thoughts, you have the power to change them. By thinking new thoughts about yourself, and choosing new courses of action, you can alter how you behave and the habits you fall into. Confidence is a skill, a thought pattern you can learn and a feeling you can generate inside. Developing a confident core is not a quick fix. You need to sustain your attention and focus not only when you're creating it but also to ensure you sustain and nurture it. Consciously choosing now to create a confident core inside empowers you to take control of your life, your goals and dreams. Don't wait on others or on any external validation to affirm what is there inside for you. Be the creator of you.

The true method of knowledge is experiment

William Blake

Part 2

Deeper Dive

In this section I'm taking you for a deeper dive into what I mean by 'your confident core'. In examining our mind–body connections, you'll build a better understanding and awareness of what is going on inside you when you feel you are confident and when you feel you're not. What lies within your sphere of influence to actively choose and control is discussed in 'question of choice'. In this section we also explore the impact your thought processes have on your physical experiences, in 'mind over matter'.

'Alchemy for the mind' is about internal transformation that subsequently leads to an external one. However the same kind of 'alchemy' can also be created by an external transformation leading to internal change. This happens when we start to think about what we look like, our personal image. This is a huge area that women (and some men) can struggle with in terms of their confidence so we end this section with an examination of personal looks and our confident core.

I do not pretend to be an expert in neuroscience or psychology. I'm a Life Coach presenting what I have learnt from my own experience and what I know has worked with my clients. For those of you who appreciate knowing what sources of information I have used in writing this book and who are interested in reading suggestions, these are listed in the resources section at the end of this book.

4

Creating a Confident Core

When I returned to work after the birth of my second child, I felt like a naked, incompetent bather in a crowded pool of expert, and appropriately dressed, swimmers. Everyone knew which way to go, following an unseen code of lane etiquette. Their stroke was refined and powerful and they seemed totally unconcerned with the presence of little old me, as I tried hard to catch up and second-guess in which direction I should be heading.

So much had changed while I had been away for that year. I was in a new office, the funding climate was radically different and the organisation was in the midst of a huge culture change. Alongside sleep deprivation, the 'normal' guilt of being a working mother and the sheer challenge of juggling the 'part time' role with two children under 5, I had to re-establish myself in work as a credible and effective player. A year is a long time to have been submersed in baby land. Despite the 'return to work' days in the last months of maternity leave, I felt raw and very unsure when I finally came back. Rationally I knew I had every reason to be confident in my abilities and skills, but those first months were emotionally exhausting. The process would have been so much smoother for everyone involved, not least for my husband who had to do *a lot* of reassurance, if I had known then the importance of building up and protecting my confident core.

Returning to work after any absence, be it for the purposes of child-care, due to illness, after a period of redundancy or perhaps bereavement, is going to feel a challenge for most. As social animals, we're very aware of the need to fit in. Childhood socialisation sees girls learning how to build rapport and boys learning about status and ranking. We like to know how and where we fit in and when you've been 'out' of a social group for a time, the cues and rules you once knew have to be re-learnt. This can be extremely challenging and can negatively impact on confidence levels that are most likely already lowered.

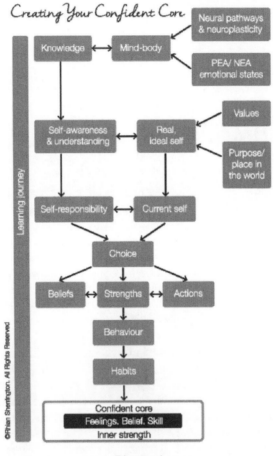

Diagram 1

Without a 'confident core', challenges such as those above can really rock your world. The same goes for the impact that specific people or situations can have on you. To help us discuss this whole concept of 'your confident core', let's take a look at Diagram One, 'Creating Your Confident Core'.

Your Confident Core

A confident core is made up of three things:
- Feelings
- Beliefs
- Skill.

Confidence is a feeling that you can achieve things and be yourself. It is a belief about yourself and your place in the world. It is also a skill that can be learnt.

Client Story

Sarah interpreted 'a confident core' as building her 'inner strength'. This is what keeps you steady when you're being shaken. It's what allows you to quickly rebuild yourself after a tsunami has washed you off your foundations. For Sarah, she realised how being made redundant three times in quick succession, followed by a spell of ME, had left her with very little 'inner strength' and self-confidence. Used to being a high achiever, with very high personal standards, she was accustomed to giving her all in her role as a regional fundraiser for a national charity. Very little room was left for a personal life. Getting married for the first time at the age of 55, her priorities suddenly shifted and with that change, she realised she now wanted a far healthier, and ultimately more rewarding, work-life balance. Her low confidence in her abilities alongside a highly self-critical perspective, however, created working habits that were not allowing her to value and protect her personal time. Since we started to work together, Sarah has identified how her feelings and beliefs about herself have been scuppering her desire to change. Working to now build her 'confident core', she's beginning to un-learn things about herself, to create new beliefs and to practise new skills. This 'inner work' will build her confidence, enable her to value her 'down time' and, ultimately, create the behaviour and habits that will enable the life balance she desires and deserves.

Diagram 1 shows how all of these feelings, beliefs and skills making up our 'inner strength' or confident core are created and nurtured by many different factors feeding into each other.

Knowledge

To know what you know and what you do not know, that is true knowledge.

Confucius

Having knowledge opens up our world. Being more knowledgeable about what is going on inside us when we do or don't feel confident helps us to understand our subsequent behaviour. Plato saw human behaviour as *'flow*[ing] *from three main sources; desire, emotion and knowledge'* (1967). Knowing more about how our mind-body connections work is a vital part of building this knowledge that leads to better self-awareness and understanding. The mind-body feedback loops and PEA and NEA emotional states are explored below and in the next chapter.

Self-awareness and Understanding

If your emotional abilities aren't in hand, if you don't have self-awareness, if you are not able to manage your distressing emotions, if you can't have empathy and have effective relationships, then no matter how smart you are, you are not going to get very far.

Daniel Goleman

An essential component of having self-awareness is having a personal vision of your real, ideal self. This enables you to acknowledge your potential, reflecting the authentic you inside, not the 'should be' or 'ought to be' person you may have been conditioned to strive towards. I've worked hard to recognise when I'm slipping into 'ought to be' and 'should be' mode. Having a good academic background, there has often been a little voice inside me saying 'you ought to be doing far better, what with all your qualifications'. At its most encouraging, this little voice has helped me to go that extra mile, to do my best when it really matters. At its worst, this 'should do' voice has made me feel highly anxious and lacking in confidence in my choices and decisions.

In studying under Professor Richard Boyatzis of Dale Western University, USA, I've come to realise how fundamental your 'ideal self' is. It encapsulates your 'personal vision', cleansed of other people's expectations of you or indeed what you perceive to be their expectations. It embodies the true authentic self that comes from finding the congruency between your values and what you believe to be your purpose in this world. Many people think they know what this is and what their values are but in truth, most people don't until they spend time really considering it. This often needs the support and perspective gained when working with a trusted other, such as with a life coach.

From a neurological perspective, thinking about the 'best of you' lights up all your positive neurology. You move into a state known as the 'positive emotional attractor' (PEA). Biological research shows that the physiological arousal of the parasympathetic nervous system (PSNS) and corresponding neuroendocrine system arouses the vagus nerve (a part of our brain) that slows down our heartbeat and triggers the release of a variety of hormones. In women, oxytocin is released; vasopressin predominately in men. This lowers feelings of anxiety, and increases feelings of tenderness and attachment to others. It calms us down and makes us feel uplifted. Research has shown that when we are in this state our cognitive performance improves, we are more emotionally open and we are more perceptive and accurate in our perception of others.

In PEA we are at our cognitive best, and I can see this process happening in front of my very eyes when working with clients on identifying their personal vision. Encouraged to set aside for a moment all the detail around how these things can happen, clients, such as Louise, become animated, ideas flow and eyes shine. For Louise, in visualising and drawing a picture of herself 10 years from now, she was encouraged to let herself see the print studio and creative business her heart truly desired. Instead of focusing on the obstacles, by asking what Laura Berman Fortgang (2001) calls 'wisdom accessing questions' (basically 'what?' not 'why'?) Louise was able to be clear on what she truly desired for herself. In this supportive PEA state her self-awareness and self understanding was considerably enhanced.

The next important step is to see the true gap between where you want to go and where you currently are — the difference between the 'ideal self' and 'current self' — and to be willing to undertake what Boyatzis calls a 'learning journey' to close the gap. Before you can do that however, you need to accept responsibility for your own life and understand that at the heart of everything lies choice.

Self-responsibility and Choice

You must take personal responsibility. You cannot change the circumstances, the seasons, or the wind, but you can change yourself. That is something you have charge of.

Jim Rohn

A statement often to be found in personal development texts points out that responsibility breaks down into two words — 'response' and 'ability'. I repeat it here as it still makes a fundamentally important point. You are *able* to *respond* to whatever is going on in your life and the way in which you choose to respond will either broaden and fulfil your life, or narrow and empty it. I've learnt about this the hard way. In my twenties, all I could do was ask 'Why me?' 'Why can't I find a loving boyfriend?' 'Why won't my boss see that I'm better than my colleague and start rewarding me accordingly?' 'Why won't my friends call me up first for a change?' 'Why is everyone else earning more money that I am?' I was on an exhausting, endless litany around the theme of 'poor me' with a subliminal theme of 'it's all their fault'. This kind of thinking, believing and behaving had me stuck until finally, just as I was turning 30, I was able to see that asking 'Why' was not serving me and l learnt to ask 'What' instead. In doing so I began to take responsibility for my own life and to slowly understand I had a choice.

> *In the long run, we shape our lives, and we shape ourselves. The process never ends until we die. And the choices we make are ultimately our own responsibility.*
>
> Eleanor Roosevelt

Calling my coaching and training business 'Choose2Flourish' has been a very deliberate act on my part. Just as we can choose how to respond to a thought or a feeling that is triggered inside our minds or bodies, we can choose whether or not to take responsibility for our lives. We can choose to take action or continue to stagnate. We can choose to strengthen and support beliefs that help and empower us and to challenge and shift those that don't. We can choose to acknowledge, use and build our strengths that allow us to expand our lives or focus instead on our weaknesses, remembering the negative stuff above the good stuff, allowing the self-critical and 'not good enough' thoughts to dominate our minds. By contrast, building a confident core that sustains and empowers requires you to step up and actively choose to flourish at work, at home, in life.

Acknowledge Strengths

Human beings are really effective at discounting the good and remembering the negative things about themselves. This amnesia over the great things we've actually achieved is all to do with our evolutionary make-up. Focusing on where we need to improve has helped us to evolve as a species, prevented us from being eaten, and enabled us to adapt to the many challenges we faced.

At the individual level, how we were brought up has a considerable influence on how easily we can tune into what we are good at but regardless of our 'starting point', we can all learn to cultivate more awareness of our strengths, and use that information to build our confidence. Knowing and 'owning' your strengths, you are less likely to be depressed or suffer low self-esteem. This really matters, especially when it comes to creating your confident core. Here's why:

1. If you know and consciously use aspects of yourself you are good at, you'll feel more positive and that in itself brings about huge benefits. For example, this includes being able to think more expansively and more creatively, as explored by Barbara Fredrickson in her 'broaden and build theory of positive emotions' (*Positivity*, 2009). This now well-accepted theory states that positivity opens our minds, making us more receptive and more creative, whilst enabling us to build new skills, new knowledge, and new ways of being.

   Fredrickson states 'positive emotions were consequential to our human ancestors because over time those good feelings broadened our ancestors' mind-sets and built their resources for the future' (2009). Working from our strengths, designing ways in which we can use more of them, more often, can be a highly successful way of bringing more positive emotions into our daily lives.

2. Knowing what our strengths are gives us a way of dealing with challenges. When you work from a place of strength, you are far more likely to be successful. As you accomplish more, you build more and more evidence of your abilities. Success breeds success, so applying your strengths to help you tackle difficult situations or conversations, for example, helps you build the self-belief and self-confidence to do more. It's a virtuous circle, which when consciously acknowledged can be very powerful.

3. Knowing what your strengths are can also help you be aware of your 'shadow' side. This is the opposite, unhelpful aspect of having that strength. For example, 'a love of excellence' has a shadow of being a perfectionist; 'optimism, zest and energy for life' (one of mine) can also lead you to overcommitting and needing to take a few reality checks. Transactional Analysis (a theory

of communication) frames someone's character traits you may find annoying as a 'strength overdone'. Developing insights to where you (and others) are perhaps overdoing some strengths can lead to better relationships, at work, at home, with friends, family and colleagues. Building this self-awareness alongside an ability to see how you can take action, supports your confident core.

4. Acting from our strengths makes it easier for us to go into 'flow' at work and find what we do more satisfying. 'Flow' has been the subject of considerable research in the field of positive psychology. One leading researcher, Mikaly Csikszentmihalyi states that flow is 'the state in which people are so involved in an activity that nothing else seems to matter' (*Flow*, 1991). Regularly experiencing flow makes you feel accomplished, competent and has a positive effect on building your confidence.

Action

Inaction breeds doubt and fear. Action breeds confidence and courage. If you want to conquer fear, do not sit home and think about it. Go out and get busy.

Dale Carnegie

At the start of every coaching session, I always ask my clients, 'How did you get on with your actions?' Eighty per cent of the time I see their eyes light up, their bodies straighten and hear a confident reply enthusing about how they've got closer to their goals through their focus and committed action. Action certainly does breed confidence and courage, but particularly so when it has been thought through and designed in such a way to push you a little out of your 'comfort zone' (where you feel completely at ease, your skill level comfortably exceeding any possible challenges) into your 'stretch zone' (where the challenge is a little more than your current skill level and your sense of ease is reduced) through small, achievable steps.

Occasionally my clients aren't so successful with their actions, due to a wide range of factors that cause a drop in motivation or an upsurge in perceived fears. You can physically see the shift this has on their self-belief and confidence and those coaching sessions are often spent boosting that confidence again, as well as ensuring the next series of action steps have a far better chance of being successfully achieved. Having the experience of exploring an alternative perspective on yourself is especially important for building self-esteem. With self-esteem, positive thinking on its own won't shift that mind-set. You need to stop negatively comparing yourself with others and take action to provide real evidence to support yourself instead.

One important key to success is self-confidence. An important key to self-confidence is preparation.

Arthur Ashe

Behaviour and Habits

We are what we repeatedly do. Excellence, then, is not an act, but a habit.

Aristotle

Behaviour is the way in which we act or conduct ourselves, especially in relation to others. It is a response to a stimulus coming from an action, our environment or from an individual or a group. Our behaviour can vary in response to physical stimuli (what we've eaten or drunk, for example), mental stimuli (what we've just seen or heard) and emotional stimuli (what we've just felt). The part of our brain that deals with processing that information is our pre-frontal cortex. The pre-frontal cortex has a lot to do (e.g. problem solving decisions, motivation, collaboration and willpower), so if behaviours get repeated a few times, a different part of the brain, the basal ganglia, engages and takes over. This controls routine activities that don't require a lot of mental attention, which can be very helpful when you consciously wish to develop a new habit. For example, as the basal ganglia likes patterns, creating and repeating a ritual around using positive affirmations can actively engage this part of brain to support you in creating a habit that builds your confidence.

However, if the new problem facing us is not exactly the same as the previous one, engaging just the basal ganglia is unlikely to help us find the solution, as it will keep on using the same old thinking patterns to try and unlock the issue. As Einstein is reputed to have said, 'doing the same thing over and over again and expecting a different result is the definition of insanity'.

The late Stephen R. Covey, one of the most widely renowned personal development experts, describes 'habit' in his best-selling book *The 7 Habits of Highly Effective People* as 'the intersection of knowledge, skill and desire'. That is, knowledge and skill provide the what, why and how to do it. The desire is the motivation, the want to do it. If we want to make something a habit in our lives, Covey argues we have to have all three. This is highly insightful when we consider what needs to happen inside our minds in order to adopt supportive, habitual ways of believing ourselves to be confident. We must be sufficiently motivated and have the knowledge and the skill to do it. With that all in place, we can create new ways of thinking and subsequently behaving.

A Word on Behaviour Change

How do you change a behaviour that is no longer serving you? This is a question that has promoted significant research, especially in public health where getting the population to stop smoking, eat more greens and take more physical activity is still a real challenge. Public health campaigns have widely used 'social marketing' to achieve this. This is an approach used to develop activities aimed at changing or maintaining people's behaviour for the benefit of the individual and society as a whole. Some of the models and theories used in public health campaigns are worth briefly reviewing as they can help us understand the stages we need to go through before we are ready, willing and able to adopt a behaviour that nurtures and nourishes our confident core.

In the 'Stages of Change' Theory, people change their behaviour through a sequence of steps:

1. **Pre-contemplation** — unaware of the need to change e.g. unaware that a lack of confidence is what is hindering them in life.

2. **Contemplation** — aware but not committed e.g. aware that they suffer from fluctuating or low confidence but don't think they are able to do anything about it or don't regard it as important enough to bother about.

3. **Preparation** — intending to change and acquiring the skills and knowledge. Acknowledging there is a problem and seeking to do something about it, such as purchasing this book.

4. **Action** — motivated now to undertake actual behaviour change, e.g. implementing the strategies described in Part III.

5. **Maintenance** — New behaviours become the norm, new habits are established. New neural pathways have been created involving the basal ganglia, through for example creating a positive preparation ritual before presenting in a meeting.

Movement through these steps isn't always a straightforward progression; you can slip back to lower steps if, for example, the environment around you changes, be it moving to a new job or a relationship breaking down. With this in mind, you can appreciate that it can take some time to adopt a new behaviour to such an extent that you've created a new habit. Research suggests between 25 and 31 days of consistently doing the new behaviour is required before the basal ganglia takes over and a habit is formed.

Becoming stressed over changing behaviour is, of course, counter productive; so let yourself evolve in a way that is comfortable for you. My only caveat is that we can get stuck for many reasons and for some time in any one of these stages of behaviour change, especially when we're on our own. So recruit support, share what you're aiming to achieve in building your confident core with your trusted friends and family. Let them support you and realise as you do how common it is to feel a lack of confidence. If that support is not available or you feel you're not moving forward, remember that this is when coaching can really help as a skilled Life Coach will enable you to 'unstick' yourself.

Another theory I want to briefly mention here is Australian behaviour change expert Les Robinson and his '5 Doors Theory', which forms a part of his 'Enabling Change' approach. He identifies 5 conditions that are needed for change to occur which I've adapted here to make them applicable to creating your confident core:

1. **Desirability** — you have to want what is offered. This is Stephen Covey's 'desire'. I also see this as you recognising and investing in your identity as the inwardly and outwardly confident person you want to be. If you don't relate to or don't have that desire, changing your behaviours is going to be very challenging. Identifying and getting clear on your 'Ideal Self' is essential.

2. **Enabling context** — this involves looking at the environmental, social, physical, institutional and even technological context of your life. All can create triggers that can have a 'push and pull' effect on your behaviour. For example, putting the kettle on for a mid afternoon cup of tea can be a trigger for reaching into the cupboard for the biscuits. Sitting down and switching your computer on at work makes you instantly look at your emails. Being with a certain person in your social group makes you put yourself down. Attending parent–teacher meetings reminds you of your miserable school days. Consider what different triggers from various 'contexts' in your life either erode or support your confident core. What can you do about these negative triggers?

3. **Can do** — this is about building your self-efficacy by lowering perceived risks and fears of action. This is a huge area of focus with my clients and we go into this in more detail in Part III.

4. **Buzz** — identify and tap into your positive motivations for change. Women are great at using their social support networks, friends and family. Generate interest and mutual support by bringing together a group who would all like to work on their 'confident core' together.

5. **Invitation** — frame an emotionally compelling invitation from a credible inviter, i.e. your future self. This is again when envisioning your future self — the 'ideal self' — is so powerful. There are a number of tools you could use to create this condition for yourself, such a writing a letter dated a year from now in which you acknowledge and appreciate all the great things you've done to create and nurture the confident core that has been built inside.

Hopefully this chapter has shown that creating a solid confident core is more than just a 'quick fix'. Only you will know how much needs to shift inside you in order to find and develop this 'inner strength'. See it though, as Diagram 1 illustrates, as a 'learning journey'. We are all on our own learning journeys in life. Comparing yours unfavourable with another is simply unhelpful. Recognise what areas on the diagram need more attention that others, prioritise what seems to be the most important aspect to work on first and take it step by step, enjoying the learning journey you are on.

5

The Mind–Body

We now appreciate that the mind and body work very closely together in a myriad of feedback loops. We know that when we are stressed, full of anxiety and fear, or depressed, our physical bodies will suffer and we run the risk of falling physically ill. Likewise when our bodies are unwell, it is very difficult to think clearly or concentrate. Our overall mood and outlook, whether we are positive and optimistic or negative and pessimistic, also affect our health and ultimately our longevity. Many studies have shown that our state of mind has a dramatic impact on our physical well-being, which in turn impacts our ability to think, make decisions and perform at our peak (Rock et al, 2009).

How our bodies function, our physiology, is intimately linked to how our brains sub-consciously, as well as consciously, respond to the stimuli around us. At the very centre is a thought, whether we are aware of it or not, that triggers our body to prepare for action. Neurons firing off in the various parts of our brain link up and spark off other neurons, creating neural pathways in the brain.

Feedback loops between thought and physiological responses in the body are generated, depending on which parts of the brain are being stimulated.

When we are in situations where we feel a lack of confidence, our emotional state, such as fear and anxiety, is interpreted by the part of the brain called the amygdala as a threat situation, triggering a physiological response in our body. The amygdala controls our basic survival instincts and kicks in very quickly in an automatic and unconscious way. As the brain cannot tell the difference between what is real and imagined, if we perceive or imagine a threat we're going to evoke the amygdala. As a consequence of the amygdala taking over, the cognitive processing part of our brain, the work of the pre-frontal cortex, is reduced, meaning our perception, processing, decision-making, motivation and collaboration all get impaired.

When a threat is perceived, the amygdala activates our sympathetic nervous system (SNS). Our body starts secreting multiple neurotransmitters such as epinephrine and norepinephrine that raise blood pressure, and cortisol, which inhibits our immune systems and the growth of new neural tissue. Blood flow gets diverted to the large muscle groups (getting ready to run). In the moment, this response can mean our body betrays our lack of confidence through becoming flushed, perspiring more or uncontrolled shaking for example, making us feel even more uncertain and out of our depth. Part of this response also involves a reduction in the flow of oxygen to the brain, so just when we need it most, we can actually see a reduction in our cognitive abilities. You may feel like you've got nothing interesting to say in situations where you don't feel very confident because actually you really don't! 'Amygdala hijack' can occur when we trigger the amygdala to arouse the SNS emotional state from a perception of threat. This is what happens, for example, when you find your heart racing at the thought of speaking to someone you find challenging.

When the stimulation of the SNS incorporates negative rather than positive emotional arousal, our mind-body state moves into what is called the 'NEA', the negative emotional attractor. This NEA state reflects the survival need of the human being, enabling us to activate ourselves and prepare to defend ourselves against threats. The amygdala stores up every perceived or real threat you have experienced since birth and uses that information to process what needs to be avoided and what can be approached. Studies have shown that a NEA state can be triggered by just one of the following factors:

- when we feel something is important,
- when something is uncertain, and
- when we feel people are watching and evaluating us.

The more important, the more uncertain and the more people involved or the longer the period of time involved, the greater the level of stress we experience and the longer the NEA continues to dominate our physiology. No wonder stress is quite rightly seen as a modern-day killer epidemic in our society — we are all under considerable bombardment of chronic stressors that can, if we don't find ways to dampen down the NEA state, lead to life-threatening illness, including depression and cardiovascular disease. Add low confidence and its associated emotional states into the mix and you can begin to appreciate why building your confident core is not just a 'nice-to-have' luxury but a fundamental tool to improve your health and well-being.

Activating Positive Emotions

The amygdala is also involved in what is called the 'reward system' and when reward is perceived rather than threat, it stimulates a change in our body's physiology by releasing 'feel-good' hormones. Instead of the SNS being triggered, our parasympathetic nervous system (PSNS) is aroused. This slows our heart rate and releases a variety of hormones, including oxytocin, (primarily in women) and vasopressin, (primarily in men), both of which are associated with many physiological, psychological and social benefits, such as being more co-operative and more altruistic. We are more perceptually open and accurate in our perceptions of others, and our cognitive processes and performance improves. No wonder then, that when you feel confident, you *are* able to step up and perform at your best, whether that be making a presentation or holding your own in an argument.

This mind-body state is called the 'positive emotional attractor' or PEA. Our bodies naturally regulate between PEA and NEA. Once a threat has gone, we switch out of NEA and move once more back into PEA. This is because being in NEA for too long is exhausting and our bodies don't just want to 'survive', but also to 'thrive', according to Barbara Fredrickson (2009). It is essential for us to have a balance between the two so that we can enjoy a sense of well-being, as well as having the ability to learn. If the PEA is stimulated too much, that person may not pay attention to threats or misunderstand their meaning. If the NEA is overly stimulated, many dysfunctional aspects of chronic SNS arousal can occur, leading to cognitive, perceptual and emotional impairment. A balance needs to be established but in order to overcome the increased virulence of negative emotions, this is a balance where the positive, the PEA, should be overemphasised (Boyatzis, Smith & Blaize, 2006).

One major way in which we can do this is through developing the personal vision and 'ideal self' described at the start of Part II. We come back to this point of being mindful and active in cultivating a positive mental attitude in Chapter 7, Mind Over Matter. When we are trying to intentionally change something about ourselves, such as being more confident, we run the risk of failing if we don't have sufficient drive and the fullest intrinsic motivation for the desired end result. Hopefully by now you can see why creating a confident core is so valuable and essential for you. Consider how many aspects of your life could improve if you did commit the time and energy. I hope that 'intrinsic motivation' for change is growing inside you as you continue reading these pages.

I've gone into some detail here on the mind–body connections and feedbacks so that you develop an appreciation of the physical and chemical processes triggered by your thoughts and perceptions. When you believe yourself to lack confidence in certain situations or with certain people, the fear and anxiety behind that perception triggers the amygdala to kick off the SNS and go into a NEA emotional state. Once in that state, the mix of chemical and physical reactions makes it hard for you to regain the cognitive agility, the physical calmness and presence of mind to perform at your best. As a result, you think you've found more evidence that you're not confident and a vicious circle of cause and effect is created inside you.

Alternatively, if you sincerely believed you were confident in that situation, with that person, you would remain or move into PSNS and an associated PEA emotional state. From there, you are far more likely to perform at your best and gather more evidence for yourself that you are competent, which builds your confidence in a wonderful virtuous, not vicious, circle. That leads us nicely into our next chapter, A Question of Choice.

6

A Question of Choice

Beliefs are like software programmes that keep repeating the
same commands, only beliefs are more pernicious, since they dig
deeper with every repetition.

Deepak Chopra

We all hold beliefs about our world and ourselves. These are principles, opinions or convictions that are held to be true or real without the need for proof. When a thought or idea is held as a belief, we no longer question it and as such, beliefs can influence every aspect of our lives. As personal development expert Anthony Robbins says, 'the most important opinion a person will ever hold is the one they hold about themselves'.

Up until 5 years ago I believed I was not a runner. I spent my money on gym membership, which was okay until it was a glorious day and I would find myself resenting being inside. My belief was challenged when I found myself reading a checklist on 'Are you ready for running?' in a newspaper supplement. With some surprise I realised I was saying yes to everything they listed. In a training day on values and beliefs with the Coaching Academy, where I was studying for two Diplomas in Personal Performance and Corporate & Executive Coaching, my trainers had used the analogy of a table losing its legs as a way to look at challenging limiting beliefs. Suddenly I could see how 'not being a runner' could be viewed as a table and as I read the exercise supplement, each one of the 'legs' supporting my belief was cut from under me. I was top-heavy (buy a better sports bra), I wasn't fit enough (I could walk fast for 30 minutes and not get breathless), I didn't have the right trainers (go buy some new ones) and finally, I didn't know where to run (pure self deception, I knew exactly where I could run). Realising I did want to exercise outdoors was enough to motivate me to make a start. Setting myself small, bite-sized steps, I built up to running a kilometre, then another. In 2011, I ran the Bristol 10K in a fraction over an hour, and my medal now hangs on my office door. I now believe I am a runner.

Changing this belief has been very helpful not only in losing my postnatal weight gain and helping me cultivate a healthy and inspiring physical activity routine, it has also added strength and depth to my inner core of confidence. With new supportive evidence, I can see myself as someone who does achieve new things for herself, who can turn around a belief that was limiting her life and who is successful in accomplishing things which at first felt very intimidating and unlikely. This is a fairly straightforward example, but it shows you how you can start questioning deeply held beliefs in your life that might be holding down your ability to feel confident. And it all starts with seeing that there is in fact a question of *choice* in what we want to hold on to and what we want to change or let go of.

Our beliefs are formed in childhood and adolescence. By the time we are 4 or 5, it is suggested that our life 'scripts' have been written. By 7 years old that script is fairly well polished and by 12, we are starting to act the scripts out. By the time we are adults, our self-image has been shaped by the attitudes and opinions we have received from others. Even under 'normal' and happy childhoods, we can all form a wide range of beliefs about ourselves that in adulthood start to hold us back. These can come from angry comments from parents or teachers, humiliating experiences or repeated exposure to feelings of failure. People unfortunate enough to have been exposed to verbal and physical abuse unsurprisingly often have significant and debilitating beliefs that need considerable professional support to help them resolve.

Beliefs are thought patterns running through particular neural pathways in our brains, triggering the mind–body responses discussed in Chapter 5. Often when we are caught up in the busy-ness of our lives, we don't recognise the limiting beliefs that are having such a powerful influence over us. These can often get in the way of people taking action and succeeding in the goals they set themselves. Given that accomplishment is such a vital aspect to living and enjoying a flourishing life, it is critical that you become clear on what beliefs are limiting you. As Sam Neffendorf says below, a lack of confidence is just a belief and as such, you can change it into something that is far more empowering. Working with a coach is one excellent way to bring about this transformation. The suggestions and strategies provided in Part III will also help you do this vital inner work. However, if there is something that seems deeply emotional in how it's manifesting inside you, then an alternative approach may well be worth exploring.

Emotional Freedom Techniques and Matrix Re-imprinting

In my transition into being a Life Coach and business owner, I knew there was something behind my sudden inability to speak confidently in public. I've been interested in Emotional Freedom Techniques for a while, learning the sequence that Sam Neffendorf explains in 'Strategy 8: Create Empowering Beliefs'. It wasn't until I found myself in floods of tears in a workshop Sam ran at a women's business networking group that I realised I needed to do something about it. Working together Sam and I unpicked how I had subconsciously created a belief that 'I couldn't permit myself to speak' after events surrounding my brother-in-law's suicide. This was layered upon deeper beliefs I had created when I was eleven around events surrounding the deaths of my Uncle and Grandma. Through using the Matrix Re-imprinting and EFT, I have been able to rebuild that confidence in my public speaking and have since been going from strength to strength. Here's Sam with his story.

Sam Neffendorf's Story

People that have issues around being confident often approach me, be that in the workplace, social situations, relationships or any other area of life. This typically comes along with frustration and low self-esteem, as they are continually beating themselves up through their internal dialogue. Yet, the concept of not being confident is nothing more than a limiting belief and as such, can be re-programmed into empowering belief instead.

An example of how a belief about confidence could arise might be as simple as this. Let's say that a little boy, from age five, was often picked last to play on a team during games at school. Over time, this pattern would have been imprinted into that boy's subconscious mind and could be formative in creating beliefs such as 'I'm no good at sport', 'I'm always last to be chosen' or even 'People don't like me'. This could remain very well hidden as children are very adaptable, yet as that boy goes through life, it can start to manifest in many different ways, including unwillingness to apply for a job, ask someone on a date or put their self forward for anything that involves a choice about them being made. These core beliefs can be very powerful in the way in which they manifest themselves in our later lives.

The good news is that we hold no blame for our beliefs, as they are entirely created through the circumstances that we have been through. Even better news is that beliefs that are no longer serving us can be addressed and more positive beliefs created in their place. Two very effective techniques to do this are Emotional Freedom Techniques (EFT) and Matrix Re-imprinting.

EFT enables you to quickly shift beliefs by identifying how you feel about a specific belief, then focusing on that feeling in the body and using it to track down a specific memory or memories that are associated with it. Then, via a process of gently tapping on meridian points (the points that needles are stuck into in acupuncture) while repeating phrases about the feelings and memories that come up, the body's emotional response is quickly discharged. This has the, initially surprising, effect of enabling you to feel that the event or feelings are no longer relevant to you, which enables you to re-assess the belief and how true it remains to you. It is important to note that a belief doesn't have to be completely eradicated in order to make amazing changes in your life. Even a tiny change, if acted upon, has infinite possibility within it. It could just offer that tiny boost that enables you to move forwards in completely new ways. This can then cause a snowball effect of new and more positive behaviour patterns appearing.

The first time that I heard that you could resolve major issues and create consistent and permanent changes in your life simply by using your fingers to tap on a few points around your face and body, I was sceptical yet inquisitive. It was sufficient for me to look into it and book onto a foundation course in EFT. I had no idea that it would lead to me leaving the corporate rat race, losing weight easily, improving my health and creating a new life full of freedom and happiness. I had been working in financial services for many years and although I was content in many ways, this aspect of my life had never felt truly comfortable, as if I was missing a significant piece. Learning EFT and subsequently Matrix Re-imprinting was the pivotal point in my life, leading gradually to the realisation that I was truly in control of my own life, rather than being subject to whatever external circumstances came my way.

One amazing change that I have made is the ability to confidently engage in public speaking. I used to dread doing this and have avoided it for much of my life. I found that I was able to use EFT to clear my nervousness and worries about embarrassing myself in front of people and this meant that I was much more comfortable and confident in stepping up and delivering a presentation. However, I still struggled to deliver a presentation without having my whole script typed out and in my hand, even when I was totally confident with my subject matter.

With Matrix Re-imprinting, I have been able to go a step further and find the root cause of this lack of confidence. By tuning into the feelings that came up when I thought about the issue, I honed in on an event that happened when I was around eleven years old and had to do a presentation at school. The eleven-year-old me had little interest in the subject, was terribly unprepared and had rambled through what he thought was nonsense. What I didn't realise then was that this eleven-year-old me created a subconscious vow not to let this happen again. This was manifesting itself in my adult life as the requirement for notes. By clearing the emotional trauma of this memory and then giving the eleven-year-old me what he wanted, which was delivering a sparkling and interesting presentation (he changed the subject to time travel and then proved it existed by bringing the adult me into the classroom at the end of the presentation!), I was able to clear the subconscious requirement to hide behind my notes.

Matrix Re-imprinting can have even more profound effects than EFT as it enables you to not only track down the events leading to the formation of beliefs, but also to act as a coach to your younger self, a part of which is still stuck in the trauma of the original event in your subconscious mind. This allows you to clear any emotional pain that is still held and then change elements of the memory to create new, more positive beliefs and emotional states that can then change your life in surprising and delightful ways. Both EFT and Matrix Re-imprinting allow you to be very creative and can be a lot of fun as well as profoundly effective.

One of the main benefits of these techniques for anyone who wants to create a confident core inside them is that, once learned, they can be applied at any time, without requiring the presence of a practitioner to deal with day-to-day stress, anxiety and other issues. Over time, this has the cumulative effect of stripping away negativity and enabling you to live a life of increased confidence, joy and freedom. It is such a simple and powerful self-help technique that it should be in everyone's toolkit.

At the heart of 'Alchemy for the Mind' is a belief in choice. Choosing to no longer tolerate the beliefs that are undermining our confidence is incredibly empowering and your confident core responds likewise. Choosing to open our minds to the potential that there may be, at a subconscious level, hidden limiting beliefs is equally liberating. It takes courage to decide to investigate root causes, which we explore in Part III of this book. Before we head into examining practical ways in which you can create your confident core, however, we need to turn our attention to considering other means whereby we can creatively use our minds to help us thrive.

7

Mind Over Matter

We often hear calls for us to put 'mind over matter', to 'think positive' and reap all manner of fantastic rewards as a result. I used to be quite sceptical of such 'self-help' philosophies and even in the midst of the acute emotional pain of my early twenties, somehow I just couldn't get myself to pick up the very books which in hindsight would have shortened my misery. A stubborn belief that 'I can do it alone' stems back to my upbringing — I'd absorbed a self-contained Welsh Valleys influence from my Mum and the stoic Londoner from my Dad. On top of that, there has been my slow transition into adulthood. As a child, our predominant state is one of dependency — we rely on our caregivers for everything. As we move out of our teens into early adulthood, the transition is one from dependency into independence. We believe we can do it all by ourselves and we don't need anyone else.

For me, I was busy pushing for my independence whilst at the same time refusing to see my life as my responsibility, particularly in romantic relationships, which I pursued as a means to boost my self-confidence. As we get older, we naturally move through various stages of 'transition' coming to realise, and hopefully accept, that interdependency between individuals and communities, rather than independence, is a true sign of mature adulthood and a flourishing approach to life. I recommend reading William Bridges *Transitions* if this is an area of interest for you.

The happiness, peace of mind and self-awareness that I am still developing in my journey has been hugely influenced and helped by the mind–body and personal development books I've now read. Working with my clients, I again see the powerful effect that 'mind over matter' can have, which is why I've included it here as a vital aspect in creating a confident core. Using positive thinking and creating a positive vision of our life and ourselves arouses the PEA emotional state. As I've described already, this sets up our brain for neurogenesis (new cell growth) and for new neural pathways to be created. Nicky Marshall has a very personal experience that demonstrates this to you, so I hand you over now to Nicky to tell her story.

Nicky Marshall's Story

I had the benefit growing up of a very wise Mother. She always taught me the benefits of thinking positive and one of her oft-used phrases was 'Mind over Matter'. Back then I never really paid much attention, but as I've got more and more into a holistic approach to life and adopted well-being techniques, this has really struck a chord with me.

Mind over Matter is the idea that by focusing our mind our physicality can change — our health, the people around us, as well as the circumstances we encounter. I love the phrase, 'When we start to look in a different way the things we look at change.' The experiences we encounter depend on the way we view them. For example if you wake up late as your alarm didn't go off, trip over the cat on your way to the bathroom and burn the toast, you declare to yourself that you are having a bad day. The mind then looks for proof to further establish this thought and you notice the heavy traffic on the way to the office, the lack of parking, the enormity of your workload, the pimple on your chin... you get my meaning. When you change your state and declare to yourself on waking that this will be a good day, your attention will be drawn to the good things. Both good and bad always exist, however you have tuned your frequency to only noticing those things that increase your wellbeing.

A few years back I had reason to put this thinking into practice. I opened a new business venture in April 2010 and began working hard to make it a success. At first I relished the long hours and endless duties with enthusiasm and vigour, happy to see my dream turning into reality.

Over time however, the hours didn't decrease and I couldn't see a way of getting help. I put on a brave face but inside I wondered how this had turned out to be so hard. Physically I was exhausted, but I battled silently on.

On a weekend diving trip I suffered a decompression illness — a muscular, skeletal and cerebral bend. I was taken by the coastguard to the mainland and then by ambulance to the Diver Diseases Research Centre and had 14 hours of recompression therapy. Initially my symptoms responded, but over time my body became weaker and my left arm and leg refused to function properly. I had no feeling in my left hand or arm and my leg felt wobbly, as if I was standing on jelly. A neurology appointment confirmed I had suffered a stroke. My confidence was badly affected and there were some dark times when I refused to go out, scared of falling over or having an accident at work. I had the support of my wonderful family but I felt beaten, scared and wondered if I should close my business completely.

Then I got to thinking. On my life journey I had learned a plethora of holistic therapies, trained my psychic abilities and learned positive thinking techniques. Perhaps this journey had been to help me now? I began to tell myself that I had an amazing functioning body, a brilliant life and stupendous motor skills. I looked at my functioning hand and asked the other to follow. I began to get fit (slowly) and told myself endless stories of my amazing progress. I laughed at my mishaps and took these as a sign to rest more.

Slowly but surely my body responded and in 2013 I was passed medically fit to dive again — something I thought was impossible. My fitness has continued to improve as well as my eyesight, and a skin condition I have suffered for 30 years disappeared too.

Why am I sharing this? Our thoughts become our reality. To gain more confidence and to change our circumstances we need to start with the functions of the brain. The brain cannot tell the difference between fact and fiction — so invent a story of how you would like it to be and your brain will look for evidence, however tiny, to back this story up as fact. Day by day you will naturally attract more and more circumstances that allow you to be confident and you will start to think bigger and act in a confident way.

Every day scientists are discovering new evidence to corroborate this thinking. Research on happiness, storytelling and brain function is being published as we speak. The benefits of working in this way are that we don't need to be smarter, thinner, more attractive or have a different upbringing to be confident. We can dispose of the phrase, 'I'll be happy when...' and choose to be happy now. Fake it until you make it, embellish your stories and add vibrancy and colour. Paint the most wonderful picture and soon you will be living it. Life can be easy and fun and require nothing more than a good imagination!

Mind over matter, as Nicky's story so wonderfully describes, is a powerful approach to life whether working specifically on your confidence or your whole life experience. She actively stimulated the neurogenesis required to recover from her stroke through choosing to think and behave as she did. However, a small word of caution: having a Consultant Psychiatrist in the family, I am aware of the damage that a sole focus on 'positive thinking' can have on people who suffer from severe and life-threatening mood disorders and mental illness. Just as you wouldn't seek to cure a diseased heart or broken leg by positive thinking and 'mind over matter' techniques alone, the same goes for mood disorders and mental illness. Speaking to your GP is a sensible step. The resources section at the end of this book has links to a quick online self-survey for depression and an excellent website for more information and resources around mood disorders.

8

Image and Confidence

How we look affects how we feel. Having an image of yourself that is healthy, supportive and reflects who you believe yourself to be has a significant bearing on creating a confident core. For many women (and some men), this is a really difficult and painful area, and it links right back to those beliefs you have about yourself, which we explored earlier in this section.

I, like many women, have been through my own struggles with my image. Hitting puberty early was horrible. It might seem insignificant, but all women have their stories about feeling embarrassed, humiliated even, by their body changes and this can set up a negative relationship with their bodies that can last a lifetime.

I look back on photographs of me in my late teens and can't believe I didn't see the beautiful girl that was there. I'm fortunate enough never to have experienced the severe negative image issues that Laura Doulton describes below, but I fully understand the effect that image concerns can have on confidence. A throw-away comment made to me when I started up the career ladder — 'dress for the post you want not the one you're in' — has remained highly instructive over the years but I've still dismantled my wardrobe in a panic when important meetings have been on the cards.

Believing in and having a negative self-image unsurprisingly stimulates your mind–body to enter into the NEA emotional state. As explained in Chapter 5, this creates a stress response, which includes the release of cortisol that, if sustained, is associated with illnesses such as depression and cardiovascular disease. We have the ability though, through *choosing* to believe in a positive self-image, to correct that negative and health damaging impact on ourselves. This is a powerful answer to those who think appearance issues are nothing to get hot and bothered about.

Being brought up by a mother who always cared for her appearance, I naturally went through a phase of completely disregarding what I looked like, and at that time, it worked brilliantly for me as I was totally confident in my decisions and enjoyed the freedom of allowing myself to dress how I pleased. I have friends however who have the opposite type of mum, the one who thinks makeup is the root of all evil and any concern or interest in what you look like was perceived as unhealthy, downright vain and actively discouraged. You can imagine what internal beliefs are created in both of those scenarios and the crisis it can generate when you're older. Laura sees the impact such unhelpful beliefs around our personal appearance can have on women every day. Here's her story.

Laura Doulton's Story

As an Image Consultant, I meet a wide variety of women who want help and guidance with their image. They come to me for all sorts of reasons but they all have one aim: they want to feel good about the way they look. It is incredibly important to them and almost all report back afterwards that their lives have been transformed, both in a practical and functional sense, i.e. having clothes that fit and meet the demands of their lives, but perhaps more importantly, a renewed confidence and sense of well-being.

Our perception of the way we think we look can have a huge impact on how we live our lives. If we are happy and at ease with our external image, we tend to feel confident interacting with others and facing a myriad of social or work-related situations. If we feel unhappy with the way we look, however, we tend to want to hide, withdraw from others and generally find social and work situations quite challenging. Worse still, our unhappiness with our appearance can turn into self-hatred and isolation. Indeed, the catalyst behind why I started my Image Consultancy business has been overcoming my own battle with negative body image.

I've been incredibly lucky to have a wonderful husband and friends who have helped me on my journey to overcoming my self-hatred.

Women take on negative thoughts about the way they look for many reasons: bad parenting, bullying, hearing negative messages via the media, abuse (both physical and emotional), bereavement, divorce or negative relationships, illness, having children and body changes. A number of factors have influenced why I found myself in such a sad and unhappy place: bullying at school, a negative relationship with my father, a tendency to be a perfectionist and comparison of myself with others, as well as the normal cultural peer-group pressures and negative media I was exposed to. I now see that I began to believe a number of 'lies' about myself and the consequences were massive.

I felt ugly and literally tried to hide and avoid many social situations. I look back now at my teen years and early 20s, and see that my potential in so many scenarios was never given a chance as I just wouldn't put myself forward. I began to accept second best and felt that others would always be better than me. It was also just mentally exhausting; I was constantly battling with negative thoughts about myself. I felt unlikeable and rejected. Of course the negative feelings about the way I looked were not in isolation. I also had a negative view of my general character and capabilities. I am certain, though, that if I had had that strong belief that I was beautiful and accepted from a young age, I would have had a very different experience growing up.

I firmly believe that at the core of a woman's identity is this need to feel beautiful. Not beautiful in the world's eyes, but that we *enjoy* our femininity and individuality; that we express ourselves through the way we dress, do our hair and perhaps wear a little make-up. The amazing thing that I see again and again as I work with women through this process, is that when a women understands she is beautiful and begins to *enjoy* being beautiful, she begins to glow and radiate confidence. This in turn unlocks all that is within her; she has the confidence to interact and bare her soul to others; display her gifts and talents and generally come alive. Everyone around her then benefits from her new-found confidence. As women we are meant to feel beautiful because we then open up in every sense and what is within us is poured out.

There is a saying that what is on the inside is more important than what is on the outside, or that true beauty comes from the heart. I wholeheartedly agree. But only in the context of our culture's view of what beauty is. I believe inner and outer beauty cannot be separated, they flow in and out of each other. For me, it was only when I accepted and began to enjoy and feel confident about the way I looked that I could start to work on some of the internal emotional baggage. And in my experience of working with clients now, the evidence is too clear to ignore. We are only whole, strong and living to our full potential when we feel happy with the way we look.

It may not be fair or good, but we have to accept we live in a world where we are judged on our appearance — we all do it to some degree or other. It is vitally important that we take care of ourselves and invest in positive self-image for our own well-being and happiness, but at the same time we should understand that projecting a confident and well-turned-out image can benefit us in our social and work lives for obvious reasons. Many doors may be opened that would otherwise remain shut, and this is particularly true in a professional sense.

In this section we've explored what exactly is your confident core, examined mind–body connection, and learned about the brain science behind the potential for 'alchemy' in our minds. You've read about the importance of choice, of changing limiting beliefs and using positive thinking to manifest the confidence and life that is there for the taking. We've ended this section considering how important our personal appearance is to our confident core. Next up in the third and final part of this book are strategies, 10 of them, brought together to help you create and nurture your vital, confident core.

Part 3

Strategies

Whether you come from a council estate or a country estate, your success will be determined by your own confidence and fortitude.
Michelle Obama

9

Strategies for a Confident Core

Creating and supporting your confident core is vital for you to succeed and flourish in life. We simply cannot achieve our life's purpose and build meaning in our lives by holding back, afraid and unsure of our abilities and selves. Investing in learning new tools and skills to create new beliefs is vital. Cultivating your confident core, your 'inner strength', fundamentally makes you feel good about yourself. Imagine truly knowing that no matter what may happen, you have what it takes to rise to the challenges because you know you can trust yourself. Confidence is so much more than just 'pretending' to be confident on the outside. Learning to project confidence to fool the boss or scary associate may help you in the short term, but a sustainable, true transformation requires you to look deeply inside, with focus and intention.

Considering your confident core as 'inner strength', as described by my client Sarah, made me reflect on the similarities between the mind–body approach taken in Pilates, which builds a strong physical core, and the mind–body process of creating a 'confident core' that I have been describing here. Both are a learning process involving new knowledge,

finding your own way of working with that new knowledge, and practice
— lots of practice!

In discussing this book with my mother, she shared her story with
me, which I suddenly heard properly for the very first time. A new teaching job for my Dad when my sister and I were eight meant moving us all
from Colchester to Swansea in South Wales. After getting us settled into
our new home and primary school, my Mum, an experienced geography
teacher, started to look for work but soon discovered that getting a full-
time teaching job was not going to be straightforward. Applications went
in, interviews came and went but somehow she was never offered the
position. She picked up short-term contracts and supply work but over
two years of looking, she was never successful at the twelve interviews
she was invited to. She received lovely feedback about being in second
place but that is small consolation when all you want is a full-time teaching post.

Not unexpectedly, Mum's self-confidence was eaten away and her
mood spiralled downwards. It came to a head one day when she found
herself sitting in my Dad's office in school, where she had a short-term
contract teaching basic reading and writing skills to less able children.
In tears, she realised she couldn't face the day, simply couldn't work,
and, unable to start the day's teaching, she headed back home instead,
to retreat under the covers and close out the world. The depression that
had been circulating finally landed and as she says, 'I hit rock bottom'.

Somehow she managed to get herself into school the next day, despite the sense of acute despair. In doing so, she tapped into a seam of
courage she didn't know was there. Heading out of the staffroom, anxious about how she was going to get through the day, a small, slightly
tatty poster on the staff noticeboard suddenly caught her eye. 'Believe in
yourself!' it simply said.

That day, for Mum, the message hit home. She realised that she did
have what it takes to be successful in a job interview. She recognised that
she was an excellent teacher and that there were real reasons why she
hadn't yet been successful in getting her longed-for full-time position.
Her confident core, as diminished as it was, was found again and she approached her next job interview a different woman. She worked out what
she needed to change and improve, she learned about body language;
she identified her strengths and repeated to herself how good she was at
her job, recalling all the positive feedback she'd had from the children
she had taught and from past appraisals with her managers. Walking into
that 13th interview, she believed that the job was hers and she blew that
interview panel away. Despite there already being a strong candidate

lined up for the post, my mum, the unknown, the outsider, got the post. Re-creating that confident core made all the difference.

In Part III of *Alchemy for the Mind*, I suggest 10 practical strategies, with accompanying actions, for you to experiment with. Explore each one for yourself and see what helps you create and nurture your confident core. Some strategies are fairly straightforward to incorporate and implement, others need more time and practice before you will feel the full benefits. I'm delighted to include further tips here from Nicky Marshall, Sam Neffendorf and Laura Doulton whom you've already met in Part II.

Changing how you think in order to create new neural pathways in your mind needs repetition and persistence. Remember, confidence isn't something that we suddenly get and which then stays with us forever. Confidence can be eroded by new events in our lives. It can also be increased and developed. Stay in tune with your inner strength, your confident core, and ensure you continue nurturing yourself to be the best 'you' there can be.

Strategy 1: Get clear on what confidence means to you

If you don't know where you are going, how can you expect to get there?

Basil S. Walsh

If you are seeking something, it is vitally important you are clear on exactly what it is you are looking for.

How I define confidence may look and feel totally different from how you would. The online Oxford Dictionary states that confidence is '*a feeling or belief that one can have faith in or rely on someone or something*' or a '*feeling of self assurance arising from an appreciation of one's own abilities or qualities*'. As 'feelings' or a 'belief' therefore, only we know ourselves what that feels like or how that belief is formed and shaped inside us. Feeling confident is a 'feel-good emotion' and as we know, positive emotions trigger chemicals in the brain that help to keep us operating out of the 'parasympathetic nervous system' (PSNS). As I've described earlier, when we are in this state we are at our cognitive best as well as being able to enjoy the many physiological, psychological and social benefits, such as being more co-operative and more altruistic. When you feel confident, you *are* able to step up and perform at your best, whether that be making a presentation or holding your own in an argument.

For me, confidence feels like freedom — being able to know and trust myself that no matter the outcome, I can say, do, 'be' really 'me', in whatever situation I find myself. I feel it in my heart, in my stomach and it shines through in how I stand, speak and relate to other people.

Twenty years ago, that was incredibly hard for me to do. Whilst getting older (and wiser) can help (these things do change as we move through the different stages in our life journey), being clear on what you feel you don't have, as well as what you desire to have, is an essential building block in creating a more confident you. From that point of clarity, you can then get to work on the 'alchemy for the mind', which is based on the fact that confidence is actually a **skill** that **can be learnt**. Confidence springs from the ability to do something, which you can then look back at and say to yourself *'I gave it a go and I learned. I know I can do that again'*.

Client Story

Charlotte was thinking about returning to work after several years out raising her children. However the thought of going back into the job market was creating considerable internal turmoil. She didn't really know what she wanted to do and saw herself as someone with very little confidence. This belief that she had no confidence was colouring every aspect of looking to her future. For example, she had little confidence and trust in the ideas that were coming to her about what she could pursue as a new career.

The very first thing we needed to work on when she started her coaching with me was to open up her understanding of what confidence meant to her and to unpick *precisely* where she felt this lack of confidence in her life. We looked at how and where did confidence show up in her life and what she thought she must have in order to be confident. From that she identified that expressing herself, through using her voice, and being able to show her intelligence, were the two highest-scoring aspects that needed to be present for her to feel confident. They were also the two areas where her self-scoring levels of current satisfaction were very low. This opened up new areas of insight for Charlotte and she realised that by identifying meetings or groups that came together to discuss the things she was interested in, she would be able to find a means to practise using her voice again to express her intellectual arguments and points of view.

Excited and buoyed up by the prospect of building up her self-confidence in this way, Charlotte identified actions that involved researching groups and getting herself booked into attending one. Creating

Strategy 1: Get clear on what confidence means to you

Your Action Log	
What am I going to do? **Top Tip:** Do the 'head, heart, gut' check. Ask your head, then your heart and then your 'gut' the same question. See how the answer is slightly different each time. Listen to all three and feel which one is the most authentic and is offering you the truest guide.	
What support do I need? Who can I ask for help?	
What strengths do I have that I can use here to help me?	
What new insights do I now have that I can apply here?	

Go to www.choose2flourish.co.uk/AlchemyBonus to download your free bonus, **The Confident Alchemist Success Path.**

Building and nurturing your confident core takes time and focus. Following the **Confident Alchemist Success Path** takes the pain out of achieving that transformation. Go grab your copy now!

manageable but 'at a stretch' (that is, you're c50% comfortable with them) goals and actions is the key to putting into place firm foundations for developing your confident core.

Actions:
- Define confidence for yourself.
- Identify when you have it (or had it) and when you don't.
- Answer the following questions for yourself to help you do that:
  - What exactly are you looking for? Consider how it feels physically, in your body as well as the **feeling** you associate with having it.
  - What are you doing, saying, being?
  - What do you hear around you?
  - What exactly do you mean by 'confidence'?

Strategy 2: Identify the specifics: Find evidence

When we feel low about ourselves, it's easy for us to become very generalist. We don't see boundaries around our condition, rather we see it as an all-encompassing trend that affects us all of the time, with all sorts of people and in all situations. Feeling pessimistic suppresses the release of our feel-good hormones, such as dopamine, by releasing cortisol instead. As we now know, excessive exposure to cortisol has been linked to many diseases such as cancer, cardiovascular disease, peptic ulcers, depression and diabetes. Feeling stuck in your life because you lack the confidence to look for new solutions, to change what is no longer serving you, puts an added stress load on your body, increasing the release of cortisol and suppressing your body's abilities to renew and recover. In such a state, energy levels and motivation can be very low, making it difficult to make the shifts you desire.

When we identify the specifics and get clear about what we do want, we initiate a process inside our subconscious that starts to seek out opportunities for us to find and achieve what we want. Remember, the brain doesn't know the difference between the real and the imagined so when we get clarity on what we *do* want, not only are we triggering the positive emotional attractor, the PEA emotional state (which makes us feel great, energised, connected and purposeful), we start to subconsciously seek out ways in which we can reach our goals. Our brain also likes to see evidence of what we are doing well and nothing builds up confidence more than when there is categorical fact, especially when linked to a positive feeling of accomplishment.

We have a tendency to remember the bad and disregard the good, so seeking out, recalling and writing down 'the good stuff' is not egotistical,

Strategy 2: Identify the specifics: Find evidence

Your Action Log	
What am I going to do?	
Top Tip: Do the 'head, heart, gut' check. Ask your head, then your heart and then your 'gut' the same question. See how the answer is slightly different each time. Listen to all three and feel which one is the most authentic and is offering you the truest guide.	
What support do I need? Who can I ask for help?	
What strengths do I have that I can use here to help me?	
What new insights do I now have that I can apply here?	

Go to www.choose2flourish.co.uk/AlchemyBonus to download your free bonus, **The Confident Alchemist Success Path.**

Building and nurturing your confident core takes time and focus. Following the **Confident Alchemist Success Path** takes the pain out of achieving that transformation. Go grab your copy now!

it's helpful, supportive and nourishes your confidence. Emma, one of my regular blog readers, mentioned how she kept a 'Fantastic Me' folder on her computer at work. Whenever she got some great feedback from a client or realised she had overcome something she had found challenging, in it went, ready to read and absorb on the 'not-so-good days' that could come along and dent her confidence.

Actions:
- Get into the habit of noticing when you're thinking or saying negative and sweeping statements about yourself (e.g. 'I never know what to say', 'I could never do that', 'I always get it wrong'.). Question yourself — is that really true for me?
- Identify the specific detail around *who* and *what* makes you feel both confident and unconfident.
- Look for patterns and identify for yourself what is happening in terms of the build-up of anxiety inside or other emotions that may be responsible for triggering off your amygdala, releasing the 'fight/flight' response.
- Ask yourself, 'what's my evidence behind thinking that?'
- Look for positive examples of when you *did* say the right thing, when you did overcome something you thought you wouldn't do. That may pick up some rational evidence that might be helpful for you, but also identify the emotional benefits, the feelings from those times when you did well. In neuro-linguistic programming (NLP), much is made of having an emotional 'anchor' whereby you can recall a 'happy place' at times of stress and challenge. Keep a 'Fantastic Me' folder and feed it on a regular basis, both in your 'deposits' of 'fantastic me' moments and 'withdrawals', when you feel the need of being reminded how good you are.

Strategy 3: Name the fear that is holding you back

Human beings are hard-wired for social connection. In our early beginnings, not being part of a group literally increased the chance of an early demise if we found ourselves isolated. This need for belonging, for being accepted and fitting in, is still influencing our subconscious today. What we say and do therefore comes loaded with meaning. If we feel uncertain and lack confidence about ourselves, it becomes very difficult for us to remain true to ourselves when this challenges social norms or the group dynamics we can find ourselves in. In this instance, therefore, fear of rejection can prevent us from speaking up or taking action.

Client Story:

Lucy was rather unfortunate to be managed by a chauvinistic and sexist boss who didn't appear to rate her contributions. Moving cities for
personal reasons and taking time out for maternity leave had resulted in
Lucy taking on a role that had meant a step backwards for her. Now she
found herself in a situation where she was both frustrated by her boss's
antagonistic demeanour towards her and increasingly demoralised and
uncertain as to what she could actually do, as he was the boss. Everyone
else in the team just put up with his sexist comments and it didn't seem
the 'done' thing to complain. Her work was suffering as a result, which
was leading to further loss of confidence and poor performance.

Initially, Lucy could only think of ways in which her boss had to
change, not her. As we can't change others, only ourselves, by helping
Lucy unpack her fears over speaking her mind, she was able to see
small ways in which she could expand her 'sphere of control'. Slowly
she developed techniques to exert herself through actions that built
her confidence rather than place her in a head-to-head situation which
she felt could be potentially very damaging. Over the course of the
four months we worked together, her confidence and trust in herself
expanded in leaps and bounds and the relationship with her boss shifted
into something far more supportive and positive, all through how she
chose to change.

Another common fear that underpins a lot of confidence issues is
a fear of failure, something that can be wired into us in childhood by
teachers or parents who don't make it okay for us to learn from our
mistakes. A fear of failure can be crippling, paralysing us from realising
opportunities to grow, accomplish and expand in our life. Unpacking a
fear of failure requires us to look fairly and squarely at the reality of the
situation and explore what we can do to both increase our chances of
a successful outcome and get comfortable at sitting with the risk and
change that expanding out of our comfort zone brings.

Actions:
- When you think of an issue or area where you feel you are lack-
  ing confidence, ask yourself: what are you afraid of? Be honest
  and look deep.
- Ask yourself whether that fear is a real or a perceived risk for
  you.
- What assumptions are you making?
- What is the worst that can happen?

- How likely is that?
- How could you reframe it so that a positive way of managing the fear is found?

Strategy 4: Act As If

One strategy I often use with my clients is to encourage them to notice who they admire.

Who exhibits the kind of behaviours you aspire to?

Who can be a confidence role model for you?

Once they have found somebody, we consider what specifically makes their role model appear confident. The list often includes things like;

- She walks and stands 'tall'.
- He shakes my hand firmly but without crushing my fingers.
- She makes eye contact with everyone sitting around the table.
- His smile always seems genuine.
- She has a very open body language — you don't feel she is shutting you out or is feeling defensive by folding her arms.
- He never apologises when someone doesn't like his idea, only when he has actually made a mistake.
- She speaks clearly, making statements not questions.

From that, my client is encouraged to consider what she is doing in similar situations and an action plan to shift towards using these subtle, but powerful, behaviours is put into place, often to considerable effect. A key part of such action is noticing the shift in *feeling* inside when these new behaviours are adopted. You begin to understand how changing your physical state, your poise, stance, depth and rate of breathing, for example, actively changes your emotional state and makes you feel more confident. When you achieve this state change, you are re-programming your mind into believing you *have* more confidence by giving it the *experience* of being confident.

Your mind doesn't know the difference between the real and the imaged — which is why anyone who has a vested interest in high performance always invests heavily in mental preparation, in the visualisation of a successful outcome. Top athletes rigorously go through an imaged sequence of themselves performing at their best. Top presenters, speakers, leaders and the like all practise the same craft — vivid visualisations that combine the successful action with how it feels. In

Strategy 3: Name the fear that is holding you back

Your Action Log	
What am I going to do? **Top Tip:** Do the 'head, heart, gut' check. Ask your head, then your heart and then your 'gut' the same question. See how the answer is slightly different each time. Listen to all three and feel which one is the most authentic and is offering you the truest guide.	
What support do I need? Who can I ask for help?	
What strengths do I have that I can use here to help me?	
What new insights do I now have that I can apply here?	

Go to www.choose2flourish.co.uk/AlchemyBonus to download your free bonus, **The Confident Alchemist Success Path.**

Building and nurturing your confident core takes time and focus. Following the **Confident Alchemist Success Path** takes the pain out of achieving that transformation. Go grab your copy now!

terms of alchemy, as our mind does not know the difference between real and imagined, we can use imaged sequences to familiarize our mind with how being confident in certain situations, with certain people, will be. What we are actually doing is creating new neural circuits that help guide future behaviour. Getting really familiar with how we want to behave, how we want to come across and react, we arouse hope which in turn stimulates the parasympathetic nervous system (PSNS) with a resultant increase in openness, cognitive power and flexibility. By mentally rehearsing in this way, we also avoid triggering the amygdala and kicking off the chances for 'amygdala hijack' (as described in Part II, chapter 5) from occurring.

Body language influences not just the impact we have on people around us, it also has a powerful effect on our physiology and how we subsequently feel and behave. As social researcher Amy Cuddy has discussed in her highly popular TED lectures, the online platform for 'ideas that change the world', adopting a power pose prior to going into a job interview or giving a presentation is a powerful way to release helpful hormones that will improve your performance in such stressful situations. Standing for three minutes in a power pose, e.g. feet wide apart, hands on hips, whilst repeating a positive affirmation or mantra about the situation you're about to enter, has been proven to make you feel more confident, assured and calmer. Such body language also has the effect of making others around you perceive you are confident, calm and competent.

Action Step:
- Rehearse in detail the situations where you believe yourself to lack confidence. If you're making a presentation, for example, run through in your mind a confident you making that presentation. Bring to life in your mind's eye how you walk, stand, appear to the audience. Imagine yourself delivering the talk in a confident, clear voice, smiling and engaging with the audience. Bring a depth of feeling and emotion to the scene.
- How do you feel, how does the audience feel?
- Bring intensity and colour, really 'live' the experience and give your mind a blueprint for how you want the actual event to follow. You'll be amazed at the transformation!
- Remember to hold a 'Power Pose' for three minutes prior to the event.

Strategy 4: Act As If

Your Action Log	
What am I going to do?	
Top Tip: Do the 'head, heart, gut' check. Ask your head, then your heart and then your 'gut' the same question. See how the answer is slightly different each time. Listen to all three and feel which one is the most authentic and is offering you the truest guide.	
What support do I need? Who can I ask for help?	
What strengths do I have that I can use here to help me?	
What new insights do I now have that I can apply here?	

Go to www.choose2flourish.co.uk/AlchemyBonus to download your free bonus, **The Confident Alchemist Success Path.**

Building and nurturing your confident core takes time and focus. Following the **Confident Alchemist Success Path** takes the pain out of achieving that transformation. Go grab your copy now!

Strategy 5: Be active, eat well and enjoy your appearance

When you look good, you feel good. Confidence in what you are wearing is very important. When you feel good, you will always perform your best without worrying about anything.

Maria Sharapova

Many of us can hide behind a façade of 'I don't mind what I look like, it isn't really important. It's the real me inside that counts.' Well, yes, the real person inside is what counts, but how you think you look does impact on how you feel — which, as we know, has huge effects on your mind and body — and your confidence. What you look like therefore *is* important and you can nurture your confident core by building in daily activity, healthy eating habits and a positive approach to your mirror.

Having a healthy body weight through enjoying the right kinds of foods and physical activity is going to nourish and energise you, as well as build your confident core. There are plenty of well-researched books and support out there if you recognise this as an area you need to work on to improve your confidence. Recognising where you are in the 'stages of behaviour change' (see chapter 4) and asking yourself what you can do about moving yourself forwards may be a very useful starting point. Outlined below are two areas where you can choose to take action: your eating and activity habits and your personal appearance.

Actions:

1. Energy In; Energy Out:
- Get clear on what you are currently doing — what is your 'current self'?
- Keep a food and physical activity diary for a week and jot down what you're consuming and how active you are. Be honest with yourself and include short bouts of activity, such as taking the stairs or working in the garden.
- Think back to Part II and especially the information on 'ideal self' and behaviour change. What is your 'ideal self'? Get specific on weight or dress size, how and when you are being active, what healthy habits you have incorporated into your day.
- How are you going to get from where you are to where you want to be?
- Prioritise where you are going to start — either the easiest things to start changing or what seems most important — and set

Strategy 5: Be active, eat well and enjoy your appearance

Your Action Log	
What am I going to do?	
Top Tip: Do the 'head, heart, gut' check. Ask your head, then your heart and then your 'gut' the same question. See how the answer is slightly different each time. Listen to all three and feel which one is the most authentic and is offering you the truest guide.	
What support do I need? Who can I ask for help?	
What strengths do I have that I can use here to help me?	
What new insights do I now have that I can apply here?	

Go to www.choose2flourish.co.uk/AlchemyBonus to download your free bonus, **The Confident Alchemist Success Path.**

Building and nurturing your confident core takes time and focus. Following the **Confident Alchemist Success Path** takes the pain out of achieving that transformation. Go grab your copy now!

yourself small, manageable steps that build success. New habits have the best chance of being created when hitched up to existing ones. So try adding on an 'healthy' action to something you already do, say a 1 minute 'plank' exercise whilst you're waiting for the kettle to boil for your first cup of tea of the day or drinking a glass of water instead of reaching for the biscuit tin and waiting 5 minutes to see if you really were hungry.

2. Love Your Image (by Laura Doulton):
Think about your lifestyle and what you need your clothes to do for you. How much of your life is assigned to work, socializing, leisure time etc.?

Think about your personality in connection with your clothes. You will always feel most confident when you are true to yourself, not the trends. Are you someone who likes to always feel comfortable and look natural with a love of the outdoors? do you like to be a bit more dramatic or make a statement? do you long to feel feminine and girly? Perhaps make a mood board and get in touch with what it is you like in clothing and accessories.

Understand your colouring, the way your eyes, skin-tone and hair colour affects which colours you look best in. It is amazing how well and vibrant you can look when wearing the right combinations of colours, even without make-up!

Understand your body-shape. Depending on your body frame and build you will look best in certain styles of clothing. Everyone can look amazing in their clothes no matter how much they think their body shape is not the 'ideal'. Again, it makes a dramatic difference when you understand what suits you and you stick to it! Our body shape can influence our style personality and how we choose to express ourselves through our clothes. My clients find it very liberating to embrace their shapes and connect their body-shape to their style personality.

Put it all together and build a hard-working capsule wardrobe that meets the demands of your lifestyle (work, leisure, social) and takes all the confusion and stress out of getting dressed in the morning. My clients love the fact that they have a wardrobe full of clothes that they know suit them, with pieces that all interchange and work together to create several different outfits for any occasion.

Invest in yourself by visiting an image consultant. There is an art and a skill to dressing well and feeling good about ourselves. We aren't necessarily born with these skills and it makes sense to learn them from an expert!

Strategy 6: Connect to Who You Really Are

How well do you really know 'you'?

What is important to you in your life?

How are you honouring that in your life?

What are your real values?

What are your strengths?

How do you use your strengths to bring accomplishment and meaning, two fundamental pillars of flourishing, into your life?

Lots of questions which we need to know the answers if we are going to be successful in creating a confident core inside ourselves.

Why?

Because intimately knowing ourselves, that self that sits deep inside, away from any negative programming we may have picked up and incorporated into our life stories, helps us find the inspiration and motivation to soar above the fears and limiting beliefs that can keep us stuck. Knowing what the 'best of me' looks and feels like opens us up to the possibility of being that person. When we know exactly who we are, then we know what is important to us, and what we have to have in our lives in order to feel happy, satisfied and successful.

Stop and reflect on that for a moment. If you knew who you really are, what's truly important to you and how you are living your life around those values and sense of meaning, how would that affect how confident you feel? Hopefully that resonates with you and you can see how you might use that awareness, that connection, to explore new ways of being and believing to create a confident core inside you.

Being the opposite, not knowing who we really are, can be highly stressful. Our lives are full of stressors — squabbling children, traffic delays, unreasonable demands and so on — which on their own can activate the sympathetic nervous system (SNS), our flight/ fight response, when we feel threatened or at risk in any way. Add to this a sense of never knowing when we're moving in the right direction, or when we're making a good decision. When we lack confidence we often don't trust ourselves, meaning we stress over the things that happen to us, what we said, what other people said. We add to this heavy load of being in chronic stress.

Most of us run the risk of being in chronic stress all the time. As a result, our SNS is not being switched off or dampened down, in order to allow the restorative switch back to our parasympathetic nervous system (PSNS). We need this re-balancing to happen, as it is when our body is in this PSNS state that it can recover and renew itself.

So what can we do to help ourselves get into a mind–body state that allows our blood pressure and pulse rate to be low and our 'feel-good' hormones to flood back into our system? Well as I've already described in Strategy 1, positive emotion does all that and we can access that positive emotion in many different ways. One way is through being able to connect to a positive vision for ourselves; of having belief in a hopeful future where we can be the 'best of me'.

Actions:
- Spend some time considering the questions at the start of this section and see what emerges for you when you return to your answers a couple of times. Doing this when you are feeling relaxed and calm is really important as it keeps the blood flowing to your brain and your mind open to new ideas and ways of thinking.
- Find and develop a relaxation practice that suits you and your lifestyle. It could be yoga, meditation, Tai Chi, mindfulness or simply going for a walk in green space or sitting quietly in a park. Find something that you regularly do where you don't think or reflect on anything at all but just 'be'. Not only does this support your health and wellbeing, you'll find the answers to these questions start to arise quite effortlessly all by their own if you give yourself a chance to stop 'doing' and 'achieving' and let things just be.

Strategy 7: Practise Being Courageous in Small Things

Aristotle once said, '*Courage is the first of human virtues because it makes all others possible*'. Having courage enables us to move through risk and uncertainty, or as Ernest Hemingway saw it, '*having grace under pressure*'. Many personal development thought leaders, inspirational figureheads and authors have been quoted as saying how important courage is to us all living a full and meaningful life. Here are a few that have personally inspired me.

Courage is not the absence of fear. It is inspiring others to move beyond it.

Nelson Mandela

Be Brave. The next level of success always lies slightly outside your current confidence zone.

Bev James (CEO, The Coaching Academy)

Strategy 6: Connect to Who You Really Are

Your Action Log	
What am I going to do? **Top Tip:** Do the 'head, heart, gut' check. Ask your head, then your heart and then your 'gut' the same question. See how the answer is slightly different each time. Listen to all three and feel which one is the most authentic and is offering you the truest guide.	
What support do I need? Who can I ask for help?	
What strengths do I have that I can use here to help me?	
What new insights do I now have that I can apply here?	

Go to www.choose2flourish.co.uk/AlchemyBonus to download your free bonus, **The Confident Alchemist Success Path.**

Building and nurturing your confident core takes time and focus. Following the **Confident Alchemist Success Path** takes the pain out of achieving that transformation. Go grab your copy now!

One's life shrinks or expands according to one's courage.
                                                    Anais Nin

Courage is what enables us to rise above what we fear and to do it anyway. Each one of us can do this but we all have our own personal scales as to how big or small the fear or challenge to be overcome is. Recognising what is your small thing to be courageous about is vital — don't try and walk in anyone's shoes but your own!

Courage might be a virtue, but it is also an experience, a skill and a belief. Psychologists who treat people with life-limiting phobias have shown how repeated exposure to what you fear actually lowers the body's psychological fear response. Neuroscientists believe they have now identified what they call the 'courage centre' in the brain (sgACC — the subgenual anterior cingulate cortex) and early studies suggest this can override the fear response controlled by the brain's amygdala. The amygdala stays quiet so your body stays in neutral and you don't have the rapid pulse, clammy, perspiring skin or loss of mental cognition.

Having that experience of practising being courageous builds up a memory bank of positive experiences that can be recalled and drawn upon when other new, fearful situations present themselves. Developing the skill of making ourselves more courageous is possible — it just needs practice and effort. We can choose to believe whether or not we have courage, just as we can choose whether to believe we are confident or not. And the two are linked. Practising overcoming small things you find fearful gives you the evidence you need to show that you are someone who can overcome a fear. At the heart of all confidence issues is a fear, such as a fear of failure or of not being good enough. When you can see that you are someone who can overcome fear, when the evidence for that is easily accessible to you, then having courage allows you to find the confidence to be who you are, to do the things you are meant to do and fulfil your life in its entirety.

This is neuroplasticity in action. New neural pathways are being created inside the brain as we learn to change our behaviour, through changing our beliefs and our thoughts. By repetition, these new behaviours can become new habits. It can take between 25 and 31 *consecutive* days to form a new habit, for a new neural pathway to be created.

Certain conditions need to be met though for new cell growth (neurogenesis). We do need to be focused, stimulated and return regularly to that area of new learning, doing our reviewing and reflecting in a safe environment. This is exactly what a successful coaching environment provides for an individual and it is exciting to see how advances in neuroscience are

Strategy 7: Practise Being Courageous in Small Things

Your Action Log	
What am I going to do? **Top Tip:** Do the 'head, heart, gut' check. Ask your head, then your heart and then your 'gut' the same question. See how the answer is slightly different each time. Listen to all three and feel which one is the most authentic and is offering you the truest guide.	
What support do I need? Who can I ask for help?	
What strengths do I have that I can use here to help me?	
What new insights do I now have that I can apply here?	

Go to www.choose2flourish.co.uk/AlchemyBonus to download your free bonus, **The Confident Alchemist Success Path.**

Building and nurturing your confident core takes time and focus. Following the **Confident Alchemist Success Path** takes the pain out of achieving that transformation. Go grab your copy now!

supporting what we know about coaching, that it helps people successfully transform their inner and outer worlds to tremendous effect.

Actions:

- Not original by any means, but the old adage of 'do something that scares you every day' still holds true. Find something that's a little difficult for you to do, something that is a small stretch out of your comfort zone, and do it regularly. If speaking to people is something you find hard to do because of your low self-confidence, make sure you speak to the person at the till every time you go shopping, striking up a short conversation beyond merely the niceties. Or smile and say hello to every third person who passes you on the street. Whatever it is, find a few small things and practise!

Strategy 8: Create Empowering Beliefs

Beliefs have the power to create and the power to destroy. Human beings have the awesome ability to take any experience of their lives and create a meaning that disempowers them or one that can literally save their lives.

Tony Robbins

The first essential step in creating empowering beliefs that will grow and nurture your confident core is to become aware of the thoughts and beliefs you have about yourself that are eroding your confidence. Millions of thoughts pass through our minds every day, some we're conscious of, and others we're not. A shift in mood usually signals to us when we've had a thought that is upsetting to us. When you're not aware of what that was, it's worth stopping for a moment and tuning into yourself to identify what that thought actually was.

Once you are more consciously aware of your thoughts, consider how many are positive towards you and how many are not. Those that are negative are called 'limiting beliefs' as these are the ones that are holding you back. Believing you are not confident is a limiting belief in itself. Your internal dialogue, as discussed in Chapter 6, is the script that is generated from your childhood and that's been polished and perfected by all your perceived experiences ever since. Your mind does not evaluate what is true or false attitudes, it accepts it all. The mind accepts information that is consistent with your beliefs, goals and which fits in with the picture of your life. It filters out the things that seem irrelevant and which do not fit in. What you expect to happen to you often will as that is where you are putting your focus — so you might as well focus on the good stuff and not the bad!

Actions:

1. Identify and change limiting beliefs around confidence
- Ask two or three people close to you to point out or reflect back when you say things that put yourself down or knock yourself back. Write it down. When you hear yourself saying negative things, write down what you are saying as well.
- Ask yourself — what do I want instead?
- For example, if you say things like 'I'm no good at complaining, I can't do that', replace that with 'I am good about complaining about poor customer service/ bad food etc'.
- Get in touch with what that positive, confident you would feel like in those situations and make a connection between your new positive thought and the feeling in your body.
- Create and write down an affirmation beginning 'I am...' or 'I have...' around that new thought; read and repeat it to yourself on a daily basis.
- (If you find that doesn't work for you try a subtle shift by turning it into a question: Will I complain effectively about customer service? Some recent research suggests that asking yourself a question stimulates your brain to go off looking for the answers and subconsciously helps you generate the shift in perspective, and behaviour, you're looking for. Try that out for yourself). Remember a 'belief is just a thought you think over and over again' (Jack Cranfield). You're in charge of what you think, so you *can* change your limiting beliefs into empowering ones.

2. Using EFT to help with low confidence issues (by Sam Neffendorf):
(In order to use this tip, you will need to know how to use basic EFT. For more information, visit www.freedomhereandnow.com to download a Quickstart Guide to EFT.)

Think of a recent event where you felt less confident than you would have liked. Take some time to picture yourself in that event. Once you have that picture, begin tapping on your karate chop point. Notice how it makes you feel right now. Now, scan through your body and identify where you feel it the most. Hone in on that feeling and examine it. Notice the colour, the size, shape and texture of that feeling. If it had an emotion, what would it be? Now give it a score out of 10 for how intense it feels right now. Once you have it, begin tapping round the points, while describing the feeling (e.g. grey ball of resentment in my belly).

Once you have tapped round the points and taken a deep breath, notice if the feeling has changed. Repeat the round again, as many times as it takes for the feelings to disappear or simply not bother you any more. If you find that the score isn't reducing, you may need to use a more in-depth technique, such as the movie technique, described in the Quickstart Manual.

You can now apply this technique to any memories that come up, clearing them one by one. Take some time to write them all down and work through them one by one. By applying it in a methodical way, you will notice a real difference to your confidence over time.

Please note that this is a brief description of an EFT tapping technique. You should be fully conversant with EFT before using this technique and you accept full responsibility for your physical, mental and emotional health should you decide to use this technique. If you are in any doubt as to whether to use this technique, contact a qualified practitioner.

Strategy 9: Own Your Strengths

Being aware of and actively using our strengths is very important to creating a confident core, but how do you know what your strengths are? You are probably aware of some, but identifying your strengths can be tricky (partly due of course to our innate tuning into the negative and the difficulty we all have in recognising what we are truly good at!) One way is to ask yourself what strengths you have just used when you have done something you feel good about. If you have a friend or trusted colleague whom you feel can give you honest feedback (itself a real skill), you can also try asking them.

If you do ask for feedback on your strengths, it's worth noting how hard it can sometimes be to actually hear a strength being identified in you, or indeed for others to hear it said of themselves. How many times have you said yourself, 'Oh it was nothing,' or, 'the others did it, I did very little,' when being praised for something done well, whether it be at work or in your personal life. Ensure you acknowledge and 'own' the good stuff about you.

Research shows there are 24 character strengths recognised across cultures as being inherently desirable human traits. Martin Seligman has used these as the basis for his 'VIA Character Strengths Tests'

Strategy 8: Create Empowering Beliefs

Your Action Log	
What am I going to do? **Top Tip:** Do the 'head, heart, gut' check. Ask your head, then your heart and then your 'gut' the same question. See how the answer is slightly different each time. Listen to all three and feel which one is the most authentic and is offering you the truest guide.	
What support do I need? Who can I ask for help?	
What strengths do I have that I can use here to help me?	
What new insights do I now have that I can apply here?	

Go to www.choose2flourish.co.uk/AlchemyBonus to download your free bonus, **The Confident Alchemist Success Path.**

Building and nurturing your confident core takes time and focus. Following the **Confident Alchemist Success Path** takes the pain out of achieving that transformation. Go grab your copy now!

questionnaire which is available, for free, on his website http://www.
authentichappiness.org. You need to register and the questionnaire will
take about 40 minutes to fill in. That time is well spent, however, as the
results can be truly illuminating. Using your strengths in different ways
across your day nurtures your confident core, so use this information to
actively and creatively apply your strengths.

Client Story:

Trisha came to me as she was feeling very low about herself and her future. All her friends were in long-term relationships but she just seemed
to be attracting unsuitable men she wasn't that bothered about, not the
soul mate she thought she really wanted. She was also in turmoil about
her work; she was about to be made redundant as the children's nursery
she worked in was closing with the owners retiring. Part of her felt she
should be pursuing a decent job, but she wasn't sure what that should
be. Another part of her wanted to enjoy being single, free of responsi-
bilities. However, she lacked the confidence in herself to decide which
path she wanted to follow.

As part of the work we did together, Trisha started to recognise
and 'own' what she was good at. One assignment she undertook
was to keep a 'strengths log' in which she wrote down what skills
she used or activities she did that she realised she was both good
at and enjoyed. At first this felt rather egotistical and contrived, but
as she started to train her mind to notice, she began to see patterns emerging and feel the difference in herself when she was using
her strengths. This work, amongst other exercises and the coaching,
helped Trisha to grow in her own eyes and she started to see herself
as someone far more competent and confident that she had previ-
ously acknowledged. Committed to following through on her action
planning, Trisha grew into her true self with amazing results. She finished her MSc, resolved her internal conflict around her romantic
relationships and we finished working together when she set off for
Tanzania to volunteer in a children's orphanage for a year, something
she had always dreamed of doing.

Actions:
- Here's where providing evidence for the strength is so valuable.
  Next time you listen to a friend or colleague talk about something
  that went well, identify a strength they used in order to achieve
  what they did. Identify specifically what they did so when you
  then feed their use of that strength back to them, you can provide

Strategy 9: Own Your Strengths

Your Action Log	
What am I going to do? **Top Tip:** Do the 'head, heart, gut' check. Ask your head, then your heart and then your 'gut' the same question. See how the answer is slightly different each time. Listen to all three and feel which one is the most authentic and is offering you the truest guide.	
What support do I need? Who can I ask for help?	
What strengths do I have that I can use here to help me?	
What new insights do I now have that I can apply here?	

Go to www.choose2flourish.co.uk/AlchemyBonus to download your free bonus, **The Confident Alchemist Success Path.**

Building and nurturing your confident core takes time and focus. Following the **Confident Alchemist Success Path** takes the pain out of achieving that transformation. Go grab your copy now!

the evidence. See and feel how different things appear by trying it out when you don't use the evidence. For those suffering from self-esteem issues, having this evidence is crucial. Nice words can be easily discounted, but positive feedback supported by evidence is more likely to be heard.

- Collecting your evidence of where and when you have used your strengths is a great activity for building up your self-confidence and belief in your abilities. Perhaps write these in a special notebook that you keep by your bedside. A proven tool for building positivity can also double up as a means to log evidence of your strengths: 'WWW+W', or 'What Went Well and Why?' Identify three things that went well in your day and acknowledge any strengths you may have used in allowing that positive event to happen.

Strategy 10: Cultivate a confident mind-set

You are not who you currently think you are. You have far more internal power and potential than you can imagine in your wildest dreams. You are destined for great things.

Robin Sharma

All of the previous nine strategies described in this section will help develop and cultivate a confident mind-set. This final strategy is about bringing it altogether as a conscious intention.

Ask yourself this:

What do you really want in your life?

What do you really, really want?

What is your bottom line?

If you believe a lack of confidence is stopping you, then it will. If you choose to believe that you have the strengths, the motivation and the confidence to achieve what you really want, then you will. As Deepak Chopra and many other thought leaders suggest, set your intention and then become detached from how you get there. I am still learning to 'detach' from the detail but I am finding that the more I trust myself to be clear on what I want, when I know that it is aligned to and congruent with my values, my ideal self and personal vision, the more I find the confidence to let go of my need for certainty and trust it will happen. Each time I do this, positive things happen.

I know I need to nurture my confident core, as much as a gardener tends to her garden. Every now and again a limiting belief 'weed' springs up and, if I allow it, will try to spread out and take over. If I neglect my body, from too many late nights, too much sugar or not enough exercise, I get run down and poorly. If I neglect my mind by thinking I'm too busy to see my friends or failing to acknowledge how much I've achieved, then I know I run the risk of small set-backs being blown up out of proportion, and my self-belief and confidence wavers.

Being and believing you are that confident, competent and courageous individual just needs you to set that intention and allow yourself to take the sequential small steps necessary to make it happen.

Client Story

Samatha knew her lack of self-confidence was preventing her from enjoying a life above and beyond her current mum and child-minder roles. With a degree from Oxford University, she felt there was more she could be now doing work-wise but a set-back in her past and the years spent bringing up her three children had eroded her inner confidence. Together we have worked through some of the strategies described here and I gave her an early draft of this book to see what she would pick out and find useful for her situation. Here's what she says:

'I was interested in this book since I wanted to address my lack of confidence in dealing with conflicts and intellectually challenging situations. Following the strategies has made me see that what confidence really means (to me) is *being myself* (Strategy 1). This created an immediate shift in my conversations with others. By concentrating on and rehearsing what this authentic confidence feels like (Strategy 3) — the relaxed breathing, poised shoulders and taking a moment to say what I really mean — I am now enjoying talking with others, even in situations outside of my comfort zone.

'Hardest for me has been overcoming fear: of the unknown, of looking stupid, of failure! Challenging myself to 'do something that scares me every day' (Strategy 7) has been really helping so far — and after 31 days I hope to have made this a habit.

'The descriptions of the brain and how we can *relearn* how to respond have inspired me to feel that I can make real changes and I am enjoying the confidence that this is bringing me.'

Actions:

1.Create your 'Belief Statement'

One exercise that never fails to nurture my clients' confidence and self-belief is to write their 'Belief Statement'.

- Write a list of all the reasons why you believe you will have the life of your dreams. Include your skills, strengths, talents, education, philosophies, experiences, personal traits, passions etc.
- Use 'I' and write in complete sentences.
- Keep writing until you run out of things to put down. Notice your feelings and emotions start to flow as you write.
- Stop, take a break for a few hours, or overnight and then come back to this exercise and start writing again.
- Repeat three times. This does two things. First, taking a break and then returning allows you to go much deeper and uncover things that weren't right at the surface. Second, each time you continue working on this exercise, read what you have already put down. This will not only help you get into the proper mindset, it will enable you to start fully integrating everything you have written.
- Once you have completed this, write one sentence that captures the whole feeling you have from your belief statement. Write it out, read it regularly - memorise and use it!

2. Three steps to instantly change your state (by Nicky Marshall):

Step 1: Stop!
We live in a crazy world of being busy, multi-tasking and achievement. We are encouraged to look for ways of doing more. STOP! Put down your phone, move away from the rock face, sit down and breathe. Scrub out those diary appointments, hide that huge 'to do' list and take a nap! It will initially feel very wrong, but do it anyway!

Step 2: Observe
Take a good look at yourself and your environment. How does your body feel? Are your shoulders scrunched up, your neck rigid and your stomach tense? Do you have tightness in your forehead or a niggling headache? On a scale of 1–10 how much energy do you have? Do the people around you encourage you or make you feel worthless? What stories are you telling yourself that make you feel bad?

Step 3: Choose
To do nothing is still a choice but a wasted one — choose to do something! Add 5 minutes' relaxation to your day or eat more nutritious food. Take up a new hobby, vary your route to the office and add more colour to your wardrobe. Change your state and your confidence will naturally re-appear!

Strategy 10: Cultivate a confident mind-set

Your Action Log	
What am I going to do? **Top Tip:** Do the 'head, heart, gut' check. Ask your head, then your heart and then your 'gut' the same question. See how the answer is slightly different each time. Listen to all three and feel which one is the most authentic and is offering you the truest guide.	
What support do I need? Who can I ask for help?	
What strengths do I have that I can use here to help me?	
What new insights do I now have that I can apply here?	

Go to www.choose2flourish.co.uk/AlchemyBonus to download your free bonus, **The Confident Alchemist Success Path.**

Building and nurturing your confident core takes time and focus. Following the **Confident Alchemist Success Path** takes the pain out of achieving that transformation. Go grab your copy now!

10

Next Steps and Your Invitation

In essence, a 'confident core' comes when there is congruence between your inner and outer life. It comes from listening, trusting and following your heart, as well as from learning to tune out and re-wire any negative thought patterns contained in your mind. That takes patience, persistence and a willingness to give up unhelpful beliefs and assumptions you may be holding.

So what next? Having read through this book, I trust you are now clearer on how much you can do in creating a confident core inside. The mind is wonderfully plastic. The advances in neuroscience, with MRI and fMRI scanning, show us that we can actually create new neural pathways when we put our minds to it. When we change our beliefs, we change our thoughts and our behaviour is more likely to follow suit. When the conditions are right, such as in a trusted coaching relationship, when you feel safe, are focused and stimulated and are encouraged to return regularly to areas of new learning (all key aspects of coaching), you can learn different behaviours, leading to new habits. Our thoughts are very powerful. How we think and what we believe about ourselves can either move us rapidly towards achieving our goals in life, or hold us back indefinitely.

The strategies and actions outlined in this book have been carefully pulled together to empower you to move forwards in developing a confident core. Doing this without support however, in isolation and away from the nurturing relationship you would enjoy with a coach, can be very challenging. No matter how good your intentions can be, we can all come across significant trials or obstacles in our path. Working with me, you get that on-going support, accountability and 'return to learning' that is so essential to re-programming your mind and creating that confident core inside you.

Clients can choose to work with me on a private, bespoke 1-to-1 basis. For those clients I feel I am able to support, I offer a complimentary 30-minute, no-obligation discovery session. Email me directly on Rhian@choose2flourish.co.uk to register your interest and to request your application form. You can also choose to work with me as part of a group programme, details of which can be found on my website, Choose2Flourish.

Thank you for reading this material. I do hope you have found it interesting, relevant and useful to your own journey in life. Remember, you *can* be the confident person you want to be.

To Your Confident and Flourishing Life!

Rhian@choose2flourish.co.uk
W: http://www.choose2flourish.co.uk
Twitter: @choose2flourish
Facebook: Choose2Flourish

Being you is the quickest way to true, sustained success. When you know what you want and find the courage to go after it, you are truly alive.

Rhian Sherrington

Resources

Books
Berman-Fortgang, L (2001) *Living Your Best Life*, Thorsons

Bridges, W. (2004) *Transitions: Making Sense of Life's Changes*, Da Cao Press, 2nd Edition

Chopra, D and Tanzi, R. E. (2012) *Super Brain: Unleash the Explosive Power of Your Mind*, Random House

Conner, J. (2008) *Writing Down Your Soul: How to Activate and Listen to the Extraordinary Voice Within*, Conari Press

Covey, S. R (2004) *The 7 Habits of Highly Effective People: Powerful Lessons in Personal Change*, Simon & Schuster UK Ltd.

Csikszentmihalyi, M. (1990) *The Psychology of Optimal Experience*, HarperCollins

Durant, W.J. (1987) *The Story of Philosophy*, Barnes & Noble

Fredrickson, B.L. (2009) *Positivity*, Three Rivers Press

Rock, D & Page, L.J (2009) *Coaching with the Brain in Mind*, Wiley

Seth, A (Editor) (2014) *30-Second Brain: The 50 most mind blowing ideas in neuroscience, each explained in half a minute*, Icon Books Ltd.

Seligman, M. (2011) *Flourish: A New Understanding of Happiness and Well-Being and how to Achieve Them*, Nicholas Brealey Publishing

Ortner, N. (2013) *The Tapping Solution: A Revolutionary System for Stress-Free Living*, Hay House

Articles & Reports
Boyatzis, R. L., Smith, M. L. & Blaize, N. 'Developing Sustainable Leaders through Coaching and Compassion', Academy of Management Learning & Education, 2006 Vol 5, No 1, 8 - 24

Boyatzis, R.L., Smith, M. L. & Oosten, E.V, 'Coaching for Change', *People Matters*, June 2010

Dunning, D. & Kruger, J. 'Unskilled and Unaware of It: How Difficulties in Recognising One's Own Incompetence Lead to Inflated Self-Assessments', *Journal of Personality & Social Psychology,* 1999, Vol 77, No 6, 1121-1134

Institute of Leadership & Management (2011) Ambition and Gender Report

Other Resources
The Black Dog Institute -- a world leader in the diagnosis, treatment and prevention of mood disorders, including depression and bipolar disorder. Self Test for Depression

www.blackdoginstitute.org.au